THE MUSLIM COOKBOOK

A RETURN TO LIFE AND HEALTH

VOLUME 1

BY BRO. MIN. RASHEED D MUHAMMAD

COMPILED BY MOSQUE #27 UNDER T.H.E.M.

FORWARD AND ACKNOWLEDGEMENT BY BRO. MIN. RASHEED MUHAMMAD

FOREWARD

AS WE QUALIFY OURSELVES FOR THE NEW WORLD THAT IS NOW MERGING IN ON THE OLD, WE MUST PREPARE OURSELVES FOR WHAT LIES AHEAD.

THIS PREPARATION IS A SPIRITUAL, MENTAL AND PHYSICAL WORK OF STRIVING TO BRING MIND, BODY AND SOUL INTO BALANCE, WHILE ALSO MAKING CONCERTED EFFORTS TO HEAL THE BODY AND MIND DAMAGED UNDER THE ATMOSPHERE OF YAKUB.

"To live a long time, Allah, in the Person of Master Fard Muhammad, has taught me life must begin with the type of food that will prolong life. We have been talking about bread. There are people so poor they have no choice, and there are some so rich who still have no choice."---pg. 9, How To Eat To Live

TO HELP YOU TO RETURN TO LIFE AND HEALTH, WE NOW OFFER TO YOU **THE MUSLIM COOKBOOK** THAT WAS THE STAPLE OF OUR NATION PRIOR TO WALLACE D. MUHAMMAD'S EFFORTS TO DESTROY THE WORKS OF HIS FATHER, THE LAST MESSENGER OF ALLAH, THE MOST HONORABLE ELIJAH MUHAMMAD.

WE PRAY THAT YOU ENJOY.

ACKNOWLEDGEMENTS

A VERY SPECIAL THANK YOU TO BROTHER CHARLES 13X OF TEMPLE #27 UNDER THE MESSENGER. MAY YOU FOREVER REST IN ABUNDANT PEACE AND LOVE.

AN EXTRA SPECIAL THANKS TO BROTHER RASHID NASSER OF CALIFORNIA FOR PROVIDING THIS INFORMATION FOR PUBLICATION...YOU ARE MY BROTHER IN THE FAITH.

TABLE SETTING

1 THE FIRST THING TO DO IS TO SEE THAT THE CLOTH IS CLEAN AND STRAIGHT. IF PLACEMATS ARE USED, PUT ONE FOR EACH PLACE SETTING, PLACING EACH SETTING OPPOSITE ONE ANOTHER.

2 FOLD EACH NAPKIN AND PLACE ON MAT AT THE RIGHT. IF THERE ARE GUESTS PLACE SECOND LARGE NAPKIN AT THE RIGHT OF THE FIRST NAPKIN TO BE USED ON THE LAP.

3 NEXT IS THE SILVERWARE. PLACE SOUP SPOON ON FIRST NAPKIN. DINNER FORK TO THE LEFT ON SOUP SPOON, PLACE KNIFE ON THE MAT AT YOUR LEFT.

4 PUT ON THE SALT AND PEPPER. IF YOU ARE GOING TO SERVE AT ONCE, YOU MAY COMPLETE YOUR TABLE SETTING WITH A PLATE OF TOAST, CHEESE AND RELISHES, BUT IF YOU ARE NOT READY TO SERVE THEN LEAVE IT OFF UNTIL YOU ARE READY. IF THERE ARE MORE THAN 4 GUESTS, USE TWO PLATES OF TOAST.

SERVING

1 HAVE THE FAMILY OR GUEST TO COME INTO THE DINING ROOM. HAVE EACH TO STAND AT THEIR PLACE WITH THE CHAIR IN BACK OF THEM UNTIL THE PRAYER HAS BEEN SAID, THEN THEY MAY BE SEATED.

2 THE SOUP IS SERVED WITH THE DINNER PLATE UNDER THE SOUP BOWL. PLACE IT IN THE CENTER OF THE MAT IN FRONT OF THE PERSON FROM THE RIGHT.

3 AFTER THE SOUP IS FINISHED, REMOVE THE PLATE, BOWL AND SPOON. IF YOU HAVE A PLATE OF SALAD YOU MAY SERVE IT AFTER YOU REMOVE THE SOUP PLATE.

4 BRING THE FOOD IN ON EACH PLATE. MILK IS ALWAYS SERVED WITH THE DINNER. PLACE GLASS NEAR THE UPPER RIGHT HAND CORNER OF THE PLACEMAT.

5 AFTER THEY HAVE FINISHED, REMOVE BOTH DINNER AND SALAD PLATES, AND SERVE THE DESSERT. IF THE DESSERT IS CAKE OR PLATE PIE, SERVE IT ON A DESSERT PLATE WITH THE FORK TO THE RIGHT OF IT WITH THE HANDLE AND

SMALL END OF THE DESSERT FACING YOU. PLACE IT IN THE CENTER OF THE MAT AND MORE MILK MAY BE SERVED IF DESIRED.

6 WHEN DESSERT IS FINISHED, REMOVE EVERYTHING FROM THE TABLE; ALSO REMOVE CRUMBS.

7 BRING IN THE CREAM AND SUGAR FOR COFFEE. IF YOU HAVE AN ELECTRIC COFFEE MAKER, YOU MAY SERVE THE COFFEE AT THE TABLE. IF NOT, BRING COFFEE IN CUP ON A SERVING TRAY WITH A SPOON IN EACH SAUCER.

8 AFTER COFFEE IS FINISHED, REMOVE CUPS, CREAM AND SUGAR AND SERVE WATER.

9 BRING IN A PITCHER OF WATER AND GLASSES. POUR EACH A GLASS. REFILL THE PITCHER AND PUT IT ON THE TABLE.

BREADS AND STUFFINGS

WHOLE WHEAT BREAD NO. 1

2 CAKES COMPRESSED YEAST	1 TBSP HONEY
1 C WARM MILK	1 TBSP VEGETABLE SALT
3 C WATER	3 LBS WHOLE WHEAT FLOUR
	(12 CUPS SIFTED)

2 TBSP VEGETABLE SHORTENING

DISSOLVE THE YEAST IN THE WARM MILK. ADD THE WATER, SHORTENING, HONEY AND SALT. ADD THE FLOUR, ENOUGH TO MAKE A STIFF DOUGH, AND MIX THOROUGHLY. TURN OUT ON A LIGHTLY FLOURED BOARD AND KNEAD ABOUT 10 MINUTES, OR UNTIL SMOOTH AND SATINY.

PUT THE DOUGH IN A WARM GREASED BOWL, BRUSH THE SURFACE VERY LIGHTLY WITH MELTED SHORTENING TO PREVENT CRUST FROM FORMING, THEN COVER LIGHTLY AND LET RISE IN A WARM PLACE (80 DEGREES TO 85 DEGREES F.) FOR ABOUT 2 HOURS, OR UNTIL THE DOUGH IS DOUBLED IN BULK AND WILL KEEP THE IMPRESSION OF A FINGER WHEN PRESSED.

PUNCH THE DOUGH DOWN THOROUGHLY IN THE BOWL, FOLD THE EDGES TOWARD THE CENTER, AND TURN OVER SO THE SMOOTH SIDE IS ON TOP. COVER AND LET RISE AGAIN ABOUT ½ HOUR, OR UNTIL THE DOUGH HAS DOUBLED IN BULK. THEN TURN IT OUT ON THE BOARD, DIVIDE INTO THREE PARTS, AND MOLD EACH THIRD INTO A BALL. LET THE BALLS REST, CLOSELY COVERED, FOR 10 MINUTES, THEN SHAPE INTO LOAVES.

PLACE EACH LOAF IN A GREASED LOAF PAN, ABOUT 9 ½ X 5 ½ . BRUSH THE TOPS WITH MELTED SHORTENING, OVER AND LET RISE ABOUT 1 HOUR, OR UNTIL DOUBLED IN BULK. BAKE IN A HOT OVEN (375 DEG.) FOR 45 MINUTES. MAKES 3 LOAVES.

WHOLE WHEAT BREAD NO. 2

DISSOLVE 2 YEAST CAKES OR 2 PACKAGES OF DRY YEAST IN 1/3 C. LUKEWARM WATER. IN A 4 QUART KETTLE BRING TO BLOOD HEAT 2 C. MILK. ADD 3 TBSP OIL, 3 TBSP HONEY OR UNSULPHURED MOLASSES OR A MIXTURE OF BOTH. STIR IN DISSOLVED YEAST. ADD 3 C. WHOLE WHEAT FLOUR AND BEAT WELL FOR 5 MINUTES.

COVER TIGHTLY AND SET IN WARM PLACE, AWAY FROM DRAUGHT, UNTIL IT RISES TO TWICE ITS BULK. TURN OUT ON FLOURED BOARD, ADD 2 TSP SALT AND KNEAD ABOUT 10 MINUTES, UNTIL SATINY, ADDING MORE FLOUR IF NECESSARY. DOUGH SHOULD BE SOFT AND PLIABLE BUT NOT STIFF. DIVIDE IN HALF AND SHAPE INTO TWO LOAVES. PLACE IN GREASED BREAD PANS AND PUT IN WARM PLACE UNTIL LOAVES DOUBLE IN SIZE.

BAKE IN HOT OVEN, 400 DEGREES, FOR 15 MINUTES. REDUCE HEAT TO 350 DEGREES AND CONTINUE BAKING FOR 40 MINUTES. BRUSH LOAVES WITH SOFT BUTTER AND TURN OUT ON RACK TO COOL.

WHOLE WHEAT BREAD NO. 3

2 C. MILK	½ CUP HONEY
3 TBSP OIL OR BUTTER	2 TBSP ACT. DRY YEAST
1 TBSP SALT	5 ½ C UNSIFTED W. W. FLOUR

HEAT MILK TO SIMMER. DROP OIL, SALT AND HONEY INTO SIMMERED MILK AND POUR INTO LARGE MIXING BOWL. COOL TO LUKEWARM.

DISSOLVE YEAST IN 1/3 C LUKEWARM WATER (TO HASTEN YEAST ACTION, SPRINKLE WITH ½ TSP SUGAR). ADD DISSOLVED YEAST TO MIXTURE IN BOWL.

ADD 3 C FLOUR. STIR 8 MINUTES WITH ELECTRIC MIXER AT LOW SPEED; OR 300 STROKES BY HAND. ADD 2 C FLOUR AND STIR WELL.

TURN ONTO FLOURED BOARD AND KNEAD UNTIL DOUGH IS SMOOTH AND ELASTIC, KNEADING IN MORE FLOUR IF NECESSARY. (THOROUGH KNEADING DEVELOPS GLUTEN WHICH IS ESSENTIAL TO GOOD TEXTURE AND VOLUME.)

PLACE IN OILED BOWL, COVER WITH A TOWEL AND LET RISE IN A WARM PLACE UNTIL DOUBLE IN BULK (80 DEGREES TO 85 DEGREES F. FOR ABOUT 1 HOUR.)

KNEAD DOWN TO ORIGINAL SIZE, COVER AND LET RISE AGAIN.

KNEAD DOWN TO ORIGINAL SIZE, CUT IN HALF, SHAPE INTO TWO LOAVES, PLACE IN OILED BREAD PANS, COVER WITH TOWEL AND LET RISE UNTIL DOUGH BEGINS TO LIFT TOWEL.

PLACE TO BAKE IN 375 DEGREES F. PREHEATED OVEN FOR 45 MINUTES, OR UNTIL GOLDEN BROWN.

REMOVE FROM PANS AND PLACE ON WIRE RACK TO COOL.

IF SOFT CRUST IS DESIRED, BRUSH WITH CREAM OR SOFT MARGARINE.

VOLUME OF LOAVES IS SACRIFICED IF DOUGH IS ALLOWED TO RISE TOO HIGH IN PANS. ALLOW 1/3 OF RISE TO TAKE PLACE IN BAKING.

WHOLE WHEAT BREAD NO. 4

4 C WHOLE WHEAT FLOUR	1 TBSP SALT
2 C WHITE FLOUR	4 TBSP SUGAR
3 WHOLE EGGS	1 ½ C MILK
3 YEAST CAKES	½ LIQUID VEGETABLE SHORTENING

HEAT MILK TO LUKEWARM, POUR SOME OVER CRUSHED YEAST, ADD 1 TBSP SUGAR TO YEAST, LET IT RISE. SIFT FLOUR TOGETHER AND ADD ALL DRY INGREDIENTS. BEAT EGGS, PUSH FLOUR AWAY FROM SIDES OF THE BOWL. ADD IN EGGS AND HALF OIL...

WORK FLOUR INTO EGGS SLOWLY, ADD YEAST MIXTURE AND MIX WELL. ADD REST OF MILK AND BEAT ALL OF THE FLOUR IN UNTIL IT FORMS DOUGH. IF THE DOUGH IS TOO SOFT, ADD MORE WHITE FLOUR.

TURN OUT ON BOARD AND KNEAD 150 TIMES, USING THE REST OF OIL TO KNEAD THE DOUGH. PUT THE DOUGH IN OILED BOWL.

LET IT RISE DOUBLE ITS SIZE, THEN TURN IT OUT ON BOARD AND KNEAD IT AGAIN FOR 150 TIMES. LET IT RISE AGAIN DOUBLE ITS SIZE.

MAKE ROLLS OR LOAVES, PUT IN PAN TO BAKE, THEN LET RISE AGAIN.

BAKE IN 300 DEGREE OVEN UNTIL WELL BROWNED.

WHOLE WHEAT PARKER HOUSE ROLLS

2 TBSP NATURAL BROWN SUGAR

1 YEAST CAKE

3 TBSP BUTTER

¼ C LUKEWARM WATER

2 TSP VEGETABLE SALT

3 ½ C SIFTED WHOLE WHEAT FLOUR

1 C SWEET MILK

PUT SUGAR, BUTTER AND SALT INTO THE MILK AND SCALD IN A DOUBLE BOILER. COOL TO LUKEWARM. DISSOLVE THE YEAST CAKE IN THE LUKEWARM WATER AND ADD TO THE COOLED MILK MIXTURE. STIR IN ENOUGH FLOUR TO MAKE A SOFT DOUGH. WHEN LIGHT, ADD THE REMAINDER OF THE FLOUR AND MIX THOROUGHLY. TURN THE DOUGH OUT ONTO A LIGHTLY FLOURED BOARD AND KNEAD FOR 10 MINUTES, UNTIL THE DOUGH IS SMOOTH AND SATINY. FORM IT INTO A LOAF AND PLACE IN AN OILED BOWL. COVER AND LET RISE IN A WARM PLACE (80 DEGREES TO 85 DEGREES F.) UNTIL DOUBLE IN BULK ABOUT 2 HOURS.

KNEAD FOR 5 MINUTES AND LET RISE AGAIN.

ROLL ON A FLOURED BOARD TO ¼ INCH IN THICKNESS AND CUT INTO ROUNDS WITH A COOKIE CUTTER. CREASE THE CENTER OF EACH ROUND WITH A KNIFE HANDLE, BRUSH ONE HALF WITH MELTED BUTTER, AND FOLD. PLACE THE ROLLS

ON AN OILED BAKING SHEET, COVER AND LET RISE UNTIL DOUBLE IN BULK--½ TO ¾ HOUR. BRUSH WITH MELTED BUTTER AND BAKE IN HOT OVEN (400 DEGREES F.) FOR 15 MINUTES.

PUMPERNICKEL

1 YEAST CAKE	2 TSP SALT
½ C WATER, LUKEWARM	1 ½ C BUTTERMILK
3 TBSP MOLASSES	2 C WHOLE WHEAT FLOUR
3 TBSP OIL	2 C RYE FLOUR

MIX AND PROCEED AS FOR BASIC WHOLE WHEAT BREAD. MORE RYE FLOUR MAY BE ADDED IF NECESSARY. THE DOUGH SHOULD BE A LITTLE STIFFER THAN FOR WHOLE WHEAT BREAD. SHAPE INTO 2 LOAVES; BAKE IN GREASED PANS AT 425 DEGREES, 10 MINUTES; AT 300 DEGREES 50 MINUTES.

MOLASSES RYE BREAD

1 C. MILK	1 PKG YEAST DISSOLVED IN ¼ C. WATER
1 C. WATER	3 ½ C RYE FLOUR
2 TBSP BUTTER	3 CUPS WHOLE WHEAT FLOUR
1/3 C. UNSULPHURED MOLASSES	¼ C LUKEWARM WATER
1 ½ TSP SALT	

HEAT MILK TO BLOOD TEMPERATURE. ADD WATER, BUTTER, MOLASSES AND SALT; COOL TO LUKEWARM. ADD SOFTENED YEAST. STIR IN WHOLE WHEAT FLOUR AND BEAT UNTIL SMOOTH. COVER AND LET RISE UNTIL LIGHT. ADD RYE FLOUR TO MAKE A FAIRLY STIFF DOUGH. KNEAD UNTIL SMOOTH. PLACE IN A BOWL AND ALLOW TO RISE UNTIL DOUBLE IN BULK. PUNCH DOWN AND LET REST 15 MINUTES. SHAPE INTO 2 LOAVES AND PLACE IN GREASED BREAD PANS. COVER AND LET RISE UNTIL AGAIN DOUBLE IN BULK. MAKE 4 DIAGONAL SLITS IN CRUST WITH SHARP KNIFE. BAKE AT 375 DEGREES, 40 TO 50 MINUTES.

SOURDOUGH BREAD

STARTER: DISSOLVE 1 YEAST CAKE IN 2 ½ C. WARM WATER AND 1 TSP HONEY. ADD 2 C. FLOUR, OR ENOUGH TO MAKE A STIFF BATTER. BEAT WELL. STORE IN BEAN CROCK OR ENAMEL PITCHER LARGE ENOUGH TO ALLOW MIXTURE TO BUBBLE TO 4 TIMES ITS VOLUME. DO NOT USE A TIN OR ALUMINUM CONTAINER. COVER LOOSELY AND LET STAND AT LEAST 3-4 DAYS IN A WARM PLACE. STIR DOWN DAILY. WHEN ANY OF THE STARTER IS USED, IT MUST BE REPLACED WITH EQUAL AMOUNTS OF FLOUR AND WATER. KEEP STARTER AT 70 DEGREES WHEN USING DAILY. IT IS BEST WHEN ABOUT A MONTH OLD.

BREAD: 2 C. STARTER   ½ TSP SODA

2 C. FLOUR   1 TSP HONEY

1 TSP SALT   1 TBSP BUTTER

SIFT TOGETHER FLOUR, SALT AND SODA. ADD TO STARTER. MIX AND ADD BUTTER AND HONEY. DOUGH SHOULD BE THICK. TURN OUT ON FLOURED BOARD AND WORK ENOUGH ADDITIONAL FLOUR TO KEEP DOUGH FROM STICKING. KNEAD UNTIL SMOOTH. PUT IN GREASED BOWL, COVER AND ALLOW TO STAND IN WARM PLACE UNTIL NEARLY DOUBLED IN BULK. SHAPE INTO LOAF AND PUT IN GREASED BREAD PAN. BAKE AT 400 DEGREES 10 MINUTES, THEN REDUCE HEAT TO 350 DEGREES AND BAKE 35 MINUTES UNTIL BREAD IS NICELY BROWNED. TURN OUT ON RACK TO COOL.

WHOLE WHEAT EGG ROLLS

1 CAKE YEAST   1 C. LUKEWARM MILK

1/3 C. WARM WATER   3 EGGS, BEATEN

½ C. BROWN OR RAW SUGAR   3 ½ C. WHOLE WHEAT PASTRY FLOUR

½ C. OIL   1 ½ TSP SALT

DISSOLVE YEAST IN WATER. ADD SUGAR AND OIL TO MILK. STIR IN YEAST AND EGGS. ADD FLOUR AND SALT TO LIQUID MIXTURE. ALLOW TO RISE TO DOUBLE ITS

BULK. BEAT DOWN AND ADD ANOTHER ½ C. FLOUR IF NECESSARY, TO MAKE DOUGH STIFF ENOUGH TO HANDLE. SHAPE INTO ROLLS, BRUSH WITH MELTED BUTTER. LET RISE TO DOUBLE THEIR SIZE. BAKE AT 350 DEGREES ABOUT 15 MINUTES.

QUICK HOT ROLLS

2 CAKES YEAST

¼ C. LUKEWARM WATER

1 C. MILK

¼ C. OIL

1 TBSP HONEY

2 TSP SALT

2 C. WHOLE WHEAT PASTRY FLOUR

3 C. UNBLEACHED WHITE FLOUR

2 EGGS, BEATEN

DISSOLVE YEAST IN WATER. HEAT MILK TO LUKEWARM; ADD OIL, HONEY, SALT; STIR. ADD WHOLE WHEAT FLOUR; ADD YEAST AND EGGS. BEAT WELL. RAISE IN WARM PLACE 15 MINUTES. PUNCH DOWN, ADD REMAINING FLOUR AND KNEAD FOR A FEW MINUTES. PAT OUT TO 12-INCH SQUARES. PLACE ON GREASED BAKING SHEET. COVER AND LET RISE IN WARM PLACE 20 MINUTES. BAKE AT 425 DEG., 12 MINUTES.

VARIATIONS:

CRESCENT--ROLL BALL OF DOUGH INTO CIRCULAR SHAPE ABOUT ¼" THICK. CUT IN PIE-SHAPED PIECES. BRUSH WITH MELTED BUTTER AND ROLL UP, BEGINNING AT WIDE END. CURVE INTO CRESCENTS ON GREASED BAKING SHEET. LET RISE UNTIL DOUBLED.

BOWKNOTS--ROLL DOUGH UNDER HAND TO ½" THICKNESS. CUT IN PIECES ABOUT 6" LONG. TIE IN KNOTS, PLACE ON GREASED BAKING SHEET. LET RISE UNTIL DOUBLED.

CLOVERLEAF ROLLS--FORM DOUGH INTO SMALL BALLS. DIP EACH IN MELTED BUTTER OR OIL AND PLACE 3 BALLS IN EACH CUP OF GREASED MUFFIN PAN. LET RISE UNTIL DOUBLED.

FOLD 'N' TWIST--FOLD 1/3 OF DOUGH INTO 12 X 18 INCH RECTANGLE. BRUSH WITH BUTTER OR OIL. FOLD OVER IN THIRDS TO FORM RECTANGLE 12 X 6 INCHES. WITH SHARP KNIFE CUT INTO ¾ INCH WIDE AND 6 INCHES LONG. ROLL ENDS OF EACH STRIP IN OPPOSITE DIRECTIONS AND BRING TOGETHER FORMING CIRCLE. SEAL ENDS AND PLACE ON GREASED BAKING SHEET. LET IT RISE UNTIL DOUBLED.

PARKER HOUSE ROLLS--ROLL OUT DOUGH ½ INCH THICK. BRUSH WITH MELTED BUTTER. CUT WITH 3 INCH BISCUIT CUTTER. FOLD EACH ROUND IN HALF AND SEAL EDGES. PLACE ROLLS 1 INCH APART ON GREASED BAKING SHEET. LET RISE UNTIL DOUBLED.

HOT CROSS BUNS

1 C. MILK	3 C. WHOLE WHEAT FLOUR
¼ C. BUTTER OR OIL	1 TSP SALT
2 TBSP HONEY	1 TSP CINNAMON
1 CAKE YEAST	½ C. DRIED FRUIT, CUT UP
1 EGG, BEATEN	

BRING MILK, BUTTER OR OIL, AND HONEY TO BLOOD TEMPERATURE. DISSOLVE YEAST IN ¼ C. LUKEWARM WATER. WHEN MILK MIXTURE HAS COOLED. ADD YEAST AND 1 ½ C. FLOUR. LET RISE UNTIL DOUBLED. ADD FRUIT, WHICH HAS BEEN TOSSED IN REMAINING FLOUR, THEN SALT, CINNAMON AND EGG. LET RISE AGAIN UNTIL DOUBLED. KNEAD AND FORM INTO ROLLS. PLACE ON GREASED BAKING SHEET, BRUSH TOPS WITH BEATEN EGG YOLK AND BAKE ABOUT 20 MINUTES. MAKE CROSS ON TOP OF EACH ROLL WITH TIP OF SPOON, USING MIXTURE OF POWDERED MILK AND HONEY.

WHOLE WHEAT STICKY BOTTOMS: MAKE DOUGH AS FOR PARKER HOUSE ROLLS. ROLL OUT ¼" THICK AND BRUSH WITH MELTED BUTTER. MIX ¼ C. NATURAL BROWN SUGAR AND 2 TSP OF GROUND CINNAMON AND DUST THE MIXTURE OVER THE BUTTERED SURFACE. ROLL UP THE SHEET OF DOUGH. DROP A DOT OF BUTTER INTO EACH CUP OF A WELL-OILED MUFFIN TIN, THEN DUST INTO EACH

ONE ½ TSP OF THE CINNAMON AND SUGAR MIXTURE. THEN CUT THE ROLL OF DOUGH CROSSWISE INTO 1" SLICES. PLACE THE SLICES IN THE MUFFIN TINS, CUT SIDE UP. AND LET RISE UNTIL DOUBLE IN BULK--½ TO ¾ HOUR. BAKE IN A MODERATE OVEN (375 DEG.) FOR 30 MINUTES.

WHOLE WHEAT BREAD

4 CUPS WHEAT FLOUR	3 SMALL YEAST CAKES	1 ½ CUPS MILK
2 CUPS WHITE FLOUR	1 TAB. SALT	1 CUP MAZOLA OIL

HEAT MILK TO LUKEWARM, POUR SOME OVER CRUSHED YEAST, ADD 1 TAB. SUGAR TO YEAST, LET IT RISE. SIFT FLOUR TOGETHER AND ADD ALL DRY INGREDIENTS, BEAT EGGS, PUSH FLOUR AWAY FROM THE SIDES OF THE BOWL, ADD IN EGGS AND HALF OF OIL. WORK FLOUR INTO EGGS SLOWLY, ADD YEAST MIXTURE AND MIX WELL. ADD REST OF MILK AND BEAT ALL THE FLOUR IN UNTIL IT FORMS DOUGH. IF THE DOUGH IS TOO SOFT ADD MORE WHITE FLOUR, TURN OUT ON BOARD AND KNEAD IT WITH THE HEEL OF HAND FOR 150 TIMES, USING THE REST OF OIL TO KNEAD THE DOUGH. PUT DOUGH IN OILED BOWL. LET IT RISE DOUBLE IT'S SIZE, THEN TURN IT OUT ON BOARD AND KNEAD IT AGAIN FOR 150 TIMES, LET IT RISE AGAIN DOUBLE IT'S SIZE. THEN MAKE OUT ROLLS OR LOAVES, PUT IN PAN TO BAKE, LET THEM RISE, THEN BAKE IN OVEN 300 DEGREES UNTIL WELL BROWN.

DO NOT EAT BREAD FOR 24 HOURS

MUFFIN ROLLS (GLAZED)

1 YEAST	¼ CUP BROWN SUGAR	½ TEAS. SALT	½ STICK BUTTER
1 WHOLE EGG	½ CUP MILK	½ TEAS. CINNAMON	½ CUP RAISINS
1 TAB. SUGAR	2 CUPS FLOUR (SIFTED)	¼ CUP WATER	¼ CUP WHEAT FLOUR

HEAT WATER TO LUKEWARM, POUR OVER YEAST, BEAT EGGS IN BOWL ADD SUGAR, SALT, AND WARM MILK. BLEND, ADD YEAST AND MELTED BUTTER, ADD

FLOUR, A LITTLE AT A TIME, BLEND WELL, TURN OUT ON BOARD AND KNEAD FOR 5 MIN. PLACE IN OILED BOWL AND LET RISE, THEN KNEAD IT AGAIN FOR 5 MIN, LET IT RISE AGAIN, THEN ROLL IT OUT TO ABOUT ¼ INCH IN THICKNESS, THEN ADD CHOPPED RAISINS, AND SPRINKLE BROWN SUGAR AND CINNAMON OVER IT, ROLL UP IN A LONG ROLL AND CUT IT IN ABOUT ONE INCH PIECES. PUT IN MUFFIN PAN ON TOP OF A SYRUP MADE OF ½ CUP BROWN SUGAR, 2 TAB. WATER, AND 2 TAB. BUTTER, PRESS DOUGH DOWN TO FORM THE MUFFIN CUP, LET RISE AND BAKE IN OVEN 300 DEG. UNTIL BROWN, TURN OUT ONCE. <u>DO NOT EAT FOR 24 HOURS.</u>

CLOVER LEAF ROLLS

TAKE SOME DOUGH FROM A REGULAR BATCH OF DOUGH AFTER IT HAS RISEN TWICE, AND MAKE THREE ROUND BALLS LIKE LARGE MARBLES, AND PLACE THEM IN AN OILED MUFFIN PAN, LET THEM RISE AND BAKE IN OVEN 300 DEG. UNTIL BROWN. <u>DO NOT EAT FOR 24 HOURS.</u>

BEAN SOUP

(small navy beans or small red beans)

2 CUPS BEANS	1 GREEN PEPPER	BLACK PEPPER	1 TEAS. PAPRIKA
4 MED. ONIONS	3 STEMS CELERY	SALT	1/3 CUP MAZOLA OIL
1 TAB. SUGAR	1 GARLIC CLOVE	1 TEAS. SAGE	½ CAN TOMATO PASTE

<u>IF COOKING RED BEANS, TOMATO PASTE IS NOT NECESSARY</u>

SOAK BEANS OVERNIGHT. WASH, PUT IN POT, CHOP VEGETABLES, ADD ALL VEGETABLES AND SEASONINGS. ADD WATER TO WELL COVERED BEANS. COOK ON MODERATE FLAME UNTIL BEANS WILL MASH EASY TO THE TOUCH. ADD MORE BOILING WATER IF NEEDED. WHEN BEANS ARE WELL DONE, STRAIN THROUGH "FOLEY FOOD STRAINER", OR EAT THEM WHOLE, AND SERVE WITH TOAST AND CHEESE. IF SOUP IS TOO THICK, ADD A LITTLE BOILING WATER.

VEGETABLE SOUP

1 SOUP BONE OR CHICKEN NECK AND GIBLETS		¼ TEAS. PAPRIKA
1 CAN TOMATOES	½ OF PEPPER	3 MED. ONIONS
½ CUP GREEN PEAS	2 CARROTS	2 MED. POTATOES
SALT & PEPPER	DASH OF TURMERIC	DASH OF CINNAMON
1 ¼ QT WATER		

PUT SOUP BONE ON TO BOIL OR CHICKEN GIBLETS, COOK UNTIL DONE, REMOVE BONES OR CHICKEN NECKS. ADD OTHER VEGETABLES AND SEASONINGS COOK UNTIL ALL VEGETABLES ARE DONE.

BARBECUED MEATS

1 TO 3 LBS. MEAT	½ CUP CHOPPED CELERY	¼ TEAS. RED PEPPER
½ STICK BUTTER	¼ TEAS. PAPRIKA	1½ TEAS. SALT
2 MED. ONIONS	¼ TEAS. CHILI POWDER	1 TAB. VINEGAR
½ GREEN PEPPER	¼ TEAS. BLACK PEPPER	1 TAB. SUGAR
3 TAB. LEMON JUICE	3 CUPS WATER	1 CAN TOMATO SAUCE

CLEAN MEAT, AND SEASON WITH SALT AND BLACK PEPPER, PLACE IN ROASTER AND BAKE UNCOVERED IN OVEN 350 DEGREES FOR 45 MIN., TURN IT OVER HALF WAY OF BAKING TIME. THEN TAKE FIRST FOUR INGREDIENTS, PLACE IN SKILLET AND COOK FOR 10 MIN. AND ADD THE REMAINING INGREDIENTS AND COOK FOR 5 MIN., THEN POUR IT OVER THE MEAT AND CONTINUE TO BAKE IN OVEN 350 DEGREES FOR ABOUT 1½ TO 2 HOURS. TURN MEAT OVER AND BASTE EVERY FEW MIN.

BROWNED RICE

1 CUP RICE	2 CUPS COLD WATER	¼ STICK BUTTER

½ TEAS. SALT   2 DASHES OF TURMERIC

WASH RICE 3 OR 4 TIMES, RUBBING IT BETWEEN THE HANDS. DRAIN OFF WATER, MELT BUTTER IN SKILLET, ADD RICE AND BROWN. STIR IT CONTINUALLY TO KEEP FROM BURNING. ADD WATER AND SEASONINGS, COVER, LET IT SIMMER OR BOIL. LOWER THE FLAME AND STEAM UNTIL RICE IS WELL DONE. <u>DO NOT STIR RICE WHILE SIMMERING OR BOILING.</u> ADD WATER LITTLE AT A TIME UNTIL RICE IS FLUFFY DONE, ALL GRAINS TO ITSELF.

BROWN RICE WITH VEGETABLES

1 CUP RICE	½ CUP CELERY	2 CUP WATER
1 GARLIC CLOVE	1 CUP GREEN PEPPER	1 TEAS. SALT
¼ TEAS. PEPPER	1 CUP ONIONS	½ STICK BUTTER
¼ TEAS. CHILI POWDER	1 TAB. TOMATO PASTE	

BROWN ONION, PEPPER, CELERY AND GARLIC IN BUTTER FOR FIVE MIN. ADD ALL SEASONINGS, BLEND WELL. BROWN RICE AND POUR THE VEGETABLES OVER IT, ADD WATER AND STEAM RICE ON LOW FLAME UNTIL ALL GRAINS ARE TENDER AND FLUFFY.

SALADS

SUMMER SALAD: MIX EQUAL PARTS OF FINELY SHREDDED CABBAGE, SLICED TOMATOES AND SLICED CUCUMBERS. SEASON WITH LEMON JUICE, A LITTLE VEGETABLE SALT AND A BIT OF ONION. SERVE COLD.

THREE IN-ONE SALAD: FINELY SHRED EQUAL PARTS OF RAW CABBAGE, CARROTS AND CELERY. SERVE COLD AND GARNISH WITH PARSLEY OR WATERCRESS. SERVE WITH FRENCH DRESSING.

TOMATO, CUCUMBER AND CELERY SALAD: ARRANGE LETTUCE HEARTS AND TWO OR THREE SLICES OF CHILLED SLICED TOMATO. COARSELY SHRED EQUAL PARTS OF CUCUMBER AND CELERY AND SEASON WITH CHOPPED GREEN ONIONS. MIX THESE CHOPPED VEGETABLES WITH MAYONNAISE DRESSING. SERVE A LARGE SPOONFUL OF THIS MIXTURE ON THE TOMATO. SPRINKLE WITH A BIT OF PAPRIKA.

TURNIP AND CARROT SALAD: FINELY SHRED YOUNG TURNIPS AND CARROTS. TO EQUAL PARTS OF THIS ADD A LITTLE CHOPPED CELERY. MIX AND SERVE IN LETTUCE-HEART CUPS. ADD A BIT OF WATERCRESS AND SERVE WITH FRENCH DRESSING.

CARROT-RAISIN SALAD: SOAK ½ C. WASHED, SEEDED RAISINS IN ½ C. LEMON JUICE. WHEN RAISINS ARE PLUMP, COMBINE WITH 1½ C. SHREDDED CARROTS, MOISTEN WITH MAYONNAISE, AND SERVE ON LETTUCE LEAVES OR BEDS OF SHREDDED CABBAGE.

RAW CHEF'S SALAD: 2 C. SHREDDED CAULIFLOWER, ½ C. CHOPPED GREEN PEPPER, ½ C. CHOPPED WATERCRESS, 1 TSP. CHOPPED ONION OR ONION JUICE, PINCH OF VEGETABLE SALT. COMBINE ALL INGREDIENTS AND MOISTEN WITH MAYONNAISE. ARRANGE ON LETTUCE LEAVES AND SERVE WITH EXTRA MAYONNAISE.

STUFFED TOMATO SALAD: DIP FIRM TOMATO IN BOILING WATER AND HOLD OVER FIRE TO LOOSEN SKINS, PEEL AND CHILL. CUT OUT CONE-SHAPED CENTER. SCRAPE OUT REMAINING PULP AND TURN UPSIDE-DOWN TO DRAIN. PLACE ON LETTUCE LEAF AND FILL WITH ANY MEAT OR VEGETABLE MIXTURE TO WHICH

SALAD DRESSING HAS BEEN ADDED. PLACE CONE-SHAPED CORE ON TOP AS A HAT, WITH POMPOM OF CREAM CHEESE OR SALAD DRESSING.

MIXED VEGETABLE SALAD: SHRED COARSELY EQUAL PARTS OF YOUNG CABBAGE AND CELERY. TO THIS ADD CHOPPED CUCUMBER, ONION, TOMATO AND A BIT OF SWEET GREEN PEPPER. CHILL AND SERVE ON CRISP LETTUCE LEAVES WITH FRENCH DRESSING.

OLIVES ITALIAN: ALLOW RIPE OLIVES TO MARINATE OVERNIGHT IN A SMALL BOWL OF YELLOW OLIVE OIL TO WHICH HAS BEEN ADDED A CLOVE OR TWO OF GARLIC.

SPRING SALAD BOWL: CUT UP WATERCRESS TENDER LEAVES OF LETTUCE, YOUNG RADISHES, GREEN ONIONS-CHOPPED FINE, 1 LARGE TOMATO-SLICED, 2 CUCUMBERS AND 2 CARROTS FINELY SHREDDED. PUT ALL IN A SALAD BOWL AND MIX WITH FRENCH DRESSING.

FRUIT SALADS: YOU CAN MAKE DELICIOUS MIXED RAW SALADS WITH FRESH RIPE FRUITS BY GIVING ATTENTION TO FRESHNESS, TEXTURE, TASTE AND ARRANGEMENT OF THE FRUIT. THE CHOICE OF FRUITS WHICH BLEND WELL IS A MATTER OF INDIVIDUAL TASTE, LIMITED ONLY BY WHAT THE MARKET AFFORDS. THE BEST FRUITS ARE ALWAYS THOSE WHICH ARE IN SEASON, PREFERABLY THOSE RIPENED IN THE SUN. A COMBINATION OF NO MORE THAN FOUR, ONE OF WHICH SHOULD BE OF THE CITRUS GROUP, MAKES A MORE PALATABLE MIXTURE THAN THE HODGE-PODGE OF MORE FRUITS.

HERE IS PARTIAL LIST OF THE VARIETY OF MATERIALS WHICH MAY BE ADDED TO FRUITS, EITHER AS PART OF THE SALAD OR AS A GARNISH, TO LIVEN UP THE MIXTURE:

MILD CHEESE

PIMENTO

WATERCRESS

MINT-SPEARMINT, APPLE, ORANGE, ETC.

SHREDDED RIND OF ORANGE OR LEMON

CRYSTALLIZED GINGER

CANDIED PEEL

SWEET DRIED FRUITS

SOME OF THE BEST COMBINATIONS ARE LISTED BELOW, AND THEY INCLUDE THE EXCEPTIONS TO THE RULE THAT CITRUS AND SWEET DRIED FRUITS DO NOT COMBINE WELL.

APPLE AND MINT

AVOCADO AND CITRUS

BANANA AND RAISINS OR DATES

ORANGE AND RIPE BANANA

ORANGE AND BLACK MILLION FIGS

ORANGE AND ONION

PERSIMMON AND ORANGE

PEAR AND CREAM CHEESE

PINEAPPLE AND CREAM CHEESE

PINEAPPLE AND DATE

PINEAPPLE AND MINT

PINEAPPLE AND STRAWBERRY

AMONG FRUITS, ORANGE AND APPLE ARE BASIC INGREDIENTS. THEY SUPPLY SWEET JUICINESS, CRISP SUBSTANCE AND COLOR. ORANGE HAS THE ADDED ADVANTAGE OF LENDING ITSELF TO PREPARATION IN VARIOUS SHAPES--SLICES, WHOLE OR CUBED, SKINNED SECTIONS OR SMALL WEDGES CUT ACROSS THE SECTIONS FROM THE CORE OUT.

THE FLAVORS AND TEXTURES OF FRUITS ARE SO INDIVIDUAL THAT WHEN ANY MIXTURE HAS COMBINED TO MAKE A FLAVORSOME BLEND, THE MATTER OF CONSISTENCY WILL HAVE BEEN TAKEN CARE OF. THE FRUIT SHOULD BE PREPARED IN LARGE, NEAT SLICES, CUBES, WEDGES OR BALLS--AND WITH ONLY THE SHARPEST OF TOOLS--TO AVOID CRUSHING OR TEARING. INCLUDE AT LEAST ONE FRUIT WHICH WILL GIVE A TOUCH OF HARMONIZING COLOR, OR USE AS A GARNISH A FEW CHERRIES, GRAPES, BERRIES OR A SPOONFUL OF BRIGHT JELLY OR CONSERVE. ALWAYS CHILL CUT FRUIT AND DO NOT MIX UNTIL JUST BEFORE SERVING TIME.

FOR THE SAKE OF HEALTH AND TIME, DO NOT PARE FRUITS. REMOVE ONLY THAT PART OF THE COATING WHICH WILL PEEL OFF. WHEN FRUITS MUST BE PARED BEFORE USING, GIVE SPECIAL ATTENTION TO THOSE LIKE APPLES AND PEARS WHICH DARKEN ON EXPOSURE TO AIR. OXIDATION WILL BE DELAYED IF THE PIECES OF FRUIT ARE COVERED WITH ACID FRUIT JUICES--CITRUS, PINEAPPLE. OXIDATION IS A VISIBLE ILLUSTRATION OF WHAT HAPPENS TO ALL CUT FRUIT UPON EXPOSURE TO AIR.

KEEP THE FRUIT CHILLED, AND REMEMBER THAT THE LIVING VALUES OF A FRUIT START TO DIMINISH FROM THE MOMENT IT IS CUT. THAT IS WHY FRUIT JUICES SHOULD NEVER BE ALLOWED TO STAND.

<u>CREAM-CHEESE FRUIT SALAD:</u> TAKE A 3 OZ. PACKAGE OF CREAM CHEESE AND DIVIDE INTO ABOUT 6 PARTS. SHAPE EACH PIECE INTO A BALL AND ROLL IT IN MINCED PARSLEY. PILE THE BALLS IN THE HOLLOWS OF PEAR OR PEACH HALVES OR CANNED PINEAPPLE SLICES. ARRANGE IN NESTS OF LETTUCE LEAVES OR ON BEDS OF SHREDDED CABBAGE. SERVE FRENCH DRESSING IN A SEPARATE DISH.

<u>MAIN DISH SALADS:</u> ON A HOT SUMMER'S DAY, NOTHING IS SO REFRESHING AS A COLD, CRISP SALAD SERVED AS THE MAIN COURSE. MAIN DISH SALADS ARE GOOD IN COOLER WEATHER TOO, PRECEDED BY A CUP OF SOUP AND SERVED WITH PIPING HOT ROLLS. BERRIES AND FRUIT WITH CHEESE ARE THE PERFECT DESSERT.

FRESH FRUIT PLATTER: A SMALL ICE CREAM SCOOP OF COTTAGE CHEESE OR CREAM CHEESE IS A SPLENDID COMPANION FOR A FRUIT PLATTER, EITHER TOPPING THE FRUIT OR PLACED ON THE SIDE. A BOWL OF YOGURT ON THE SIDE IS ANOTHER FAVORITE COMPLEMENT. SALAD DRESSINGS WITH A TWANG OF MINT OR CHEESE ARE AN IMAGINATIVE TOUCH. HERE IS A GOOD COMBINATION AS A STARTER TO THE MANY COOL AND COLORFUL PLATTERS YOU WILL DREAM UP FOR YOURSELF.

ALTERNATE ON EACH SALAD PLATE FAN-SHAPED BANANA SLICES, WEDGES OF ORANGE, MELON BALLS, PINEAPPLE SLICES, WHOLE STRAWBERRIES, CANNED OR FRESH PEACH HALVES. GARNISH WITH SPRIGS OF WATERCRESS OR CREAM CHEESE BALLS ROLLED IN MINCED PARSLEY OR BLACK CHERRIES, PURPLE GRAPES OR RASPBERRIES. SERVE WITH YOGURT AS DRESSING, OR SWEET WHIPPED CREAM FLAVORED WITH HONEY OR MINT.

CABBAGE AND WATERCRESS SALAD: SHRED VERY FINE THE CABBAGE AND ADD A BIT OF ONION. JUST BEFORE SERVING, ADD A DRESSING OF TWO-THIRDS THICK SOUR CREAM AND ONE-THIRD LEMON JUICE WITH A BIT OF VEGETABLE SALT.

CABBAGE SALAD RUSSE: SHRED FINE YOUNG TENDER CABBAGE AND ADD 1/3 AS MUCH CHOPPED WATERCRESS. SERVE ON LETTUCE OR ROMAINE WITH FRENCH DRESSING.

FACTS ABOUT SALADS

SALADS MAY BE SERVED IN 6 DIFFERENT WAYS:

GARNISH SALADS: ARE THE SMALL AND DECORATIVE ADDITIONS TO YOUR MAIN DISH. THEY MAY BE RADISH ROSES, CARROT CURLS, SPRIGS OF PARSLEY OR WATERCRESS, LITTLE LETTUCE CUPS FILLED WITH A FRUIT OR VEGETABLE SALAD, OR TINY MOLDED GELATIN SALADS. DRESSINGS SHOULD BE USED SPARINGLY AND OUGHT TO BE PIQUANT.

APPETIZER SALADS ARE SERVED AS THE FIRST COURSE AND SHOULD LOOK AND TASTE ESPECIALLY GOOD, SINCE THEY ARE APPETITE TEASERS. KEEP THE PORTIONS SMALL. CRISP RAW VEGETABLES ARE EXCELLENT, AS ARE SEAFOOD

AND FISH SALADS, EITHER MOLDED OR PLAIN; FRUIT SECTIONS OR AVOCADO SLICES ARE ALSO FINE APPETIZER SALADS. DRESSINGS SHOULD BE ON THE TART SIDE RATHER THAN BLAND. THESE SMALL SALADS MAY ALSO BE SERVED AS HORS D'OEUVRES.

<u>MAIN-COURSE SALADS</u> CONSTITUTE THE MAJOR PART OF THE MEAL AND SHOULD THEREFORE, PROVIDE ALL THE NECESSARY NUTRIENTS. THEIR VARIETY IS LIMITLESS, INCLUDING COMBINATIONS OF COOKED OR RAW VEGETABLES WITH MEAT, POULTRY, FISH, EGGS OR CHEESE, AS WELL AS COMBINATIONS OF FRUITS AND CHEESE. MOLDED GELATIN SALADS ARE A FAVORITE MAIN COURSE FOR SUMMER LUNCHEONS.

<u>ACCOMPANIMENT SALADS</u> ARE JUST WHAT THE NAME IMPLIES. THEY ARE SERVED WITH THE MAIN COURSE AND IN GENERAL OUGHT TO BE COLD AND CRISP FOR CONTRAST. GREENS, RAW VEGETABLES AND WELL-SEASONED DRESSINGS PROVIDE A TASTE CONTRAST FOR THE REST OF THE HOT MEAL.

<u>DESSERT SALAD</u> IS USUALLY COLORFUL AND DAINTY. IT IS SERVED AS A LIGHT DESSERT FOR A MEAL, OR MAY BE THE MAIN FOOD AT A PARTY. THE DESSERT SALAD MAY BE GELATIN MOLDS OF FRUITS, FROZEN-FRUIT SALADS, FRESH FRUIT, BERRIES OR MELON.

<u>SLAWS</u> ARE OFTEN CLASSED ALONE BECAUSE THEY ARE SERVED IN SO MANY DIFFERENT WAYS, SUCH AS GARNISH, APPETIZER, MAIN DISH, ACCOMPANIMENT SALAD OR THE SALAD IN A SALAD SANDWICH. THEY ARE RED OR GREEN SHREDDED CABBAGE COMBINED WITH ANY OF THE FOLLOWING: CARROTS SHREDDED, SHREDDED APPLES OR PINEAPPLE, CHOPPED CELERY, OLIVES, GREEN PEPPERS, FRUITS OR HARD-COOKED EGGS. A SMOOTH, WELL-SEASONED DRESSING, YOGURT OR SOUR CREAM IS USED AS A BLENDER.

SALAD GREENS

GREENS ARE THE BASIS FOR ALMOST EVERY SALAD AND THEREFORE ARE MOST IMPORTANT. THE BEST ARE THOSE THAT ARE VERY GREEN, AS THEY HAVE MORE CHLOROPHYLL, VITAMINS AND MINERALS.

ROMAINE: DARK GREEN, LARGE SPEARLIKE LEAVES THAT MAY BE USED AS A BASE, A GARNISH, SERVED ALONE OR IN A TOSSED GREEN SALAD. ROMAINE HAS A SHARPER TASTE THAN LEAF LETTUCE.

LEAF LETTUCE: LONG, LOOSE, DARK GREEN LEAVES OFTEN WITH RUST COLORED CRIMPLED EDGES.

BIB LETTUCE OR BOSTON LETTUCE: IS SHAPED LIKE A GREEN ROSE. THE LEAVES ARE VERY TENDER AND MILD IN FLAVOR. THEIR CUP-LIKE LEAVES MAKE VERY PRETTY SALADS.

ICEBERG LETTUCE: IS COMPACT AND CRISP BUT, BECAUSE IT IS NOT DARK GREEN TO THE CORE, IS NOT DESIRABLE FROM A NUTRITION VIEWPOINT.

ENDIVE: HAS FLAT GREEN, TIGHTLY-CURLED LEAVES AND IS MILD TO BITTER IN TASTE. THE VERY CURLY ENDIVE HAS A WHITE CENTER. IT IS ALSO CALLED CHICORY. VERY DECORATIVE.

ESCAROLE: IS BROAD-LEAFED ENDIVE, DEEP GREEN, SHARP IN TASTE, BEST USED WHEN CHOPPED WITH OTHER GREENS.

WATERCRESS: CAN BE USED IN MANY WAYS, AS A BASIS FOR A SALAD, IN TOSSED GREEN SALAD, AS A FINGER SALAD, AS A GARNISH, OR CHOPPED IN SANDWICHES. IT IS VERY IMPORTANT FOR ITS VITAMIN AND MINERAL CONTENT, AND HAS A NIPPY FLAVOR.

SPINACH: IS BEST USED WHEN THE LEAVES ARE YOUNG, IN A TOSSED GREEN SALAD.

PARSLEY: IS USUALLY A GARNISH, BUT CAN BE CHOPPED AND SERVED IN GREEN SALADS, IN SANDWICHES OR ON HORS D'OEUVRES, AS WELL AS SPRINKLED OVER MEAT-SALADS.

MINT LEAVES: ARE USED AS A GARNISH FOR COCKTAILS, MAIN DISHES, ACCOMPANIMENT SALADS OR DESSERTS.

CELERY TOPS OR BEET TOPS: WHEN YOUNG AND TENDER ARE AN ADDITION TO POTATO SALAD, GREEN SALADS AND VEGETABLE SALADS.

SWISS CHARD: WHEN VERY YOUNG CAN BE USED IN A GREEN SALAD.

CHINESE CABBAGE: HAS LONG, WIDE LEAVES WITH A WHITE CENTER SECTION AND SOMEWHAT STRONG FLAVOR. THE STIFF WHITE CENTER CAN BE CUT OUT AND COOKED AS A VEGETABLE. FLAVOR IS LIKE CABBAGE.

NASTURTIUM LEAVES: USE AS GREEN BACKGROUND FOR FRUIT SALADS.

GREEN CABBAGE: IS OFTEN MIXED WITH GREEN SALAD, RAW VEGETABLES, FRUITS OR SERVED ALONE.

TOSSED GREEN SALADS

VARY YOUR TOSSED GREEN SALADS WITH ANY OF THE FOLLOWING:

BLEU CHEESE CRUMBLED OVER GREENS JUST BEFORE SERVING.

TOSS IN ½ TO 1 C. TOASTED BUTTERED WHOLE WHEAT BREAD CRUMBS.

GRATED CARROTS, BEETS, TURNIPS OR CABBAGE, TOSSED IN ALONG WITH DRESSING.

FOR A SIMPLIFIED CAESAR SALAD, STIR 1 EGG GENTLY AND POUR OVER GREENS, THEN ADD SMALL CUBES OF WHOLE WHEAT BREAD AND SLIVERS OF CHICKEN, VEAL OR ANCHOVY FILLETS. TOSS ALONG WITH DRESSING.

IF YOU MUST USE LEFT-OVER VEGETABLES, SUCH AS PEAS, GREEN BEANS, CARROTS OR BEETS, THEY MAY BE ADDED TO SALAD GREENS BEFORE TOSSING.

SMALL WEDGES OF TOMATO, ALTERNATED WITH SLICES OF PEELED AVOCADO MAY BE ARRANGED ON TOSSED SALAD AFTER DRESSING HAS BEEN MIXED IN.

SLICED HARD COOKED EGG OR THIN SLICES OF RADISH MAKE A GOOD TOPPING.

GRATED RAW BEETS, RED CABBAGE, YOUNG TURNIPS OR THINLY SLICED CUCUMBER, GREEN OR RED BELL PEPPERS, OR TENDER YOUNG PEAS OR STRING BEANS ARE ALL GOOD TOPPINGS FOR GREEN SALADS.

GARNISH OR APPETIZER SALADS

TOMATO FLOWERS: CHOOSE SMALL, FIRM TOMATOES. PEEL OR NOT, AS DESIRED. WITH SMALL, SHARP KNIFE, DIVIDE EACH TOMATO INTO SIXTHS OR EIGHTHS, CUTTING JUST TO THE BASE, BUT NOT QUITE THROUGH. SPREAD INTO PETALLED SHAPE AND FILL WITH DEVILLED EGG, OR MIXTURE OF MASHED AVOCADO WITH LEMON JUICE, OR YOUR FAVORITE CREAM CHEESE MIXTURE. GARNISH WITH BLACK OLIVES AND SERVE ON CRISP LETTUCE LEAVES IF DESIRED.

CHEESE APPLES: USE CREAM CHEESE, TINTED WITH RED VEGETABLE COLORING. SHAPE INTO TINY APPLES AND INSERT A FEW CLOVES AT BLOSSOM AND STEM ENDS. USE PALE GREEN COLORING AND SHAPE INTO PEARS, OR ORANGE COLORING FOR CARROTS. ARTIFICIAL COLORING OF VEGETABLE ORIGIN IS HARMLESS. DO NOT USE SYNTHETIC COLORINGS. COLOR MAY BE BRUSHED ON CREAM CHEESE INSTEAD OF BLENDED IN. EGG YOLK, HARD-COOKED AND GRATED, AND SIEVED SPINACH HAVE BEEN USED SUCCESSFULLY TO COLOR CREAM CHEESE.

CELERY CURLS: USE CRISP GREEN STALKS, FAIRLY LARGE. CUT INTO 2-INCH PIECES. MAKE LENGTHWISE SLITS, CLOSE TOGETHER, FROM BOTH ENDS OF EACH STALK, LEAVING ABOUT ½ INCH UNCUT IN CENTER. SOAK ABOUT 1 HOUR IN ICE WATER TO MAKE THE SPLIT ENDS FORM CURLS.

RADISH ROSES: CUT OFF ROOT AND STEMS ENDS. MAKE LENGTHWISE SLITS THROUGH RADISH, BUT LEAVE BOTTOM UNCUT. WITH POINT OF KNIFE, PRESS INTO OPEN PETALS. CHILL IN ICE WATER TO MAKE PETALS UNFOLD. FOR RADISH ACCORDIONS, MAKE SLITS HORIZONTALLY, ALMOST THROUGH RADISH, AND CHILL IN ICE WATER.

FRINGED CUCUMBERS: RADISHES, CARROTS OR BEETS ARE SCORED LENGTHWISE WITH A FORK, THEN SLICED.

FRENCH-CUT TOMATOES: SLICE VERY THIN, NOT HORIZONTALLY, BUT FROM STEM TO BLOSSOM END. THERE IS LESS LOSS OF JUICE AND THEY ARE EASIER TO EAT.

CARROT CURLS ARE MADE BY THINLY SCRAPING LARGE CARROTS WITH VEGETABLE PEELER. (Carrots should be at room temperature.) FASTEN WITH TOOTHPICK, PLACE IN COLD WATER TO CHILL AND SET CURL.

PITTED OLIVES MAY BE FILLED WITH CELERY OR CARROT STICKS, OR CREAM CHEESE. ROLL IN OIL TO BRING BACK SHINE.

MAYONNAISE DRESSINGS: THE SECRET OF MAKING MAYONNAISE LIES IN ADDING THE OIL GRADUALLY. AT FIRST ADD IT A DROP AT A TIME OR THE OIL WILL FLOAT ON TOP OF THE FINISHED DRESSING. DON'T GIVE UP IF THIS HAPPENS. BEAT YOUR BATCH OF DRESSING INTO ANOTHER EGG YOLK AS IF YOU WERE STARTING A NEW BATCH.

AFTER ABOUT A QUARTER OF THE OIL HAS BEEN BEATEN IN, YOU CAN ADD THE REST IN SLIGHTLY LARGER DOSES.

A WHOLE EGG CAN BE USED INSTEAD OF AN EGG YOLK, BUT IT MAKES A THINNER DRESSING.

MAYONNAISE

1 EGG YOLK

1 C. OLIVE OR VEGETABLE OIL

2 TBSP LEMON JUICE

½ TSP VEGETABLE SALT

½ TSP HONEY

SLIGHTLY BEAT THE EGG YOLK. ADD THE OIL DROP BY DROP, BEATING BRISKLY THE WHILE WITH A ROTARY EGG BEATER. AFTER THE FIRST ¼ CUP HAS BEEN BEATEN IN, YOU CAN ADD THE OIL FASTER. THIN WITH LEMON JUICE UNTIL THE DRESSING IS OF THE CONSISTENCY AND TARTNESS YOU WANT. FOLD IN THE SALT AND HONEY, STORE IN A COVERED JAR IN THE REFRIGERATOR. (DON'T LET THE JAR REST AGAINST THE FREEZING UNIT OR THE OIL WILL FLOAT TO THE TOP.)

CHEESE

MAKE YOUR OWN COTTAGE CHEESE: Cottage cheese is made by heating sour milk until the curds coagulate and separate from the watery part, the whey. You can either let the milk turn sour by itself, heat it over low heat to lukewarm, and drain through cheesecloth, or sour the milk by adding lemon juice. Put fresh milk in a saucepan, heat it gently to lukewarm, stirring with a wooden spoon, and then put into it 2 tsp. of lemon juice per cup of milk. Stir well and when the milk is thoroughly curdled, strain it through cheesecloth, pressing out the whey with wooden spoon to drain the cheese thoroughly. Flavor with a little vegetable water and vitamize it by adding chopped chives and lemon. Keep in the refrigerator.

MAKE YOUR OWN CREAM CHEESE: Take a bottle of fresh cream and let it sour, which will take about 2 days at room temperature. Pour the contents into a cheesecloth bag and let it drain. When solid, put it in the icebox and chill it, forming it into a flat cake or into balls. Delicious for desserts or cake filling.

CHEESE SOUFFLE

4 TBSP BUTTER	1 C. GRATED YELLOW CHEESE
3 TBSP WHOLE WHEAT FLOUR	5 EGGS, SEPARATED
2/3 C. MILK, SCALDED	½ TSP VEGETABLE SALT

MELT THE BUTTER IN THE TOP OF A DOUBLE BOILER. BLEND IN THE FLOUR AND GRADUALLY STIR IN THE SCALDED MILK. COOK OVER HOT WATER, STIRRING CONSTANTLY, UNTIL THICK AND SMOOTH. ADD THE GRATED CHEESE AND REMOVE FROM HEAT. BEAT THE EGG YOLKS UNTIL THICK AND LEMON-COLORED AND ADD TO THE CHEESE MIXTURE WITH THE VEGETABLE SALT. LET THE MIXTURE COOL TO LUKEWARM, THEN BEAT THE EGG WHITES UNTIL STIFF BUT NOT DRY. HAVE YOUR BAKING DISH READY AND WELL BUTTERED, YOUR OVEN HEATED. FOLD THE EGG WHITES SWIFTLY INTO THE CHEESE MIXTURE AND POUR INTO THE BAKING DISH. BAKE AT 350 DEGREES, 30 -40 MINUTES, UNTIL THE CENTER IS FIRM. SERVE AT ONCE. DELICIOUS WITH A MAN-SIZED GREEN SALAD.

CORN AND CHEESE SOUFFLE

3 TBSP BUTTER	1 1/3 C. THIN CREAM
2 TBSP MINCED GREEN PEPPER	2/3 C. GRATED YELLOW CHEESE
2 EGGS, SEPARATED	2/3 C. CORN, GRATED RAW OR CANNED
3 TBSP WHOLE WHEAT FLOUR	1 TSP VEGETABLE SALT

MELT THE BUTTER IN A SAUCEPAN. SAUTE THE PEPPER UNTIL SOFT, THEN ADD THE FLOUR. STIR UNTIL WELL BLENDED. ADD THE CREAM GRADUALLY, STIRRING UNTIL THICK AND SMOOTH. ADD THE CHEESE AND STIR UNTIL MELTED. REMOVE FROM THE HEAT AND ADD THE CORN AND SALT. BEAT THE EGG YOLKS UNTIL THICK AND LEMON-COLORED AND ADD SLOWLY TO THE CHEESE MIXTURE. LET THE MIXTURE COOL AND BEAT THE EGG WHITES STIFF BUT NOT DRY. FOLD INTO THE CHEESE MIXTURE, THEN POUR INTO A BUTTERED BAKING DISH. PLACE IN A HOT OVEN (400 DEGREES) FOR A FEW MINUTES, THEN TURN THE HEAT DOWN TO 325 DEGREES. BAKE UNTIL THE CENTER IS FIRM, ABOUT 30 MINUTES. SERVE IMMEDIATELY.

CREOLE TOAST

FOR EACH PERSON TO BE SERVED, CUT 2 OR 3 SLICES OF RIPE TOMATO. PUT EACH SLICE ON THE BUTTERED SIDE OF A SQUARE OF BREAD CUT SLIGHTLY LARGER THAN THE TOMATO SLICE. PUT THESE INTO A VERY HOT OVEN (400 DEGREES) FOR 5 OR 10 MINUTES. THEN ADD TO EACH SLICE A SPRINKLING OF MINCED ONION, MINCED GREEN PEPPER, A DASH OF VEGETABLE SALT, AND PAPRIKA. ON TOP PUT A THICK LAYER OF GRATED AMERICAN CHEESE AND RETURN TO THE OVEN TO BAKE UNTIL THE CHEESE AND BREAD ARE BROWNED.

CREAM CHEESE ICING FOR CAKES

1 3OZ. PACKAGE CREAM CHEESE	1/8 TSP VEGETABLE SALT
¼ C. FRUIT JUICE OR HEAVY CREAM	2½ C. NATURAL BROWN SUGAR

SOFTEN THE CREAM CHEESE WITH A FORK AND WORK IN THE FRUIT JUICE OR THE CREAM. ADD THE VEGETABLE SALT AS YOU WORK, THEN GRADUALLY STIR IN THE SUGAR UNTIL THE CONSISTENCY OF THE ICING IS RIGHT FOR SPREADING. BEAT UNTIL CREAMY AND SPREAD OVER THE CAKE.

LOW-CALORIE STUFFED CELERY

1/3 C. HOOP CHEESE OR FARMER-STYLE COTTAGE CHEESE   ½ TSP MARJORAM

1 TBSP MAYONNAISE   DASH OF TABASCO

½ TSP SALT   4-6 CRISP STALKS OF CELERY

MIX CHEESE AND MAYONNAISE TOGETHER, ADD SEASONINGS AND WHIP UNTIL SMOOTH. STUFF CELERY STALKS. SERVE WITH SALADS, OR CUT IN 1-INCH PIECES AND SERVE AS APPETIZER.

LOW-CALORIE CHEESE-RICE CASSEROLE

2 TBSP MINCED ONION   1 C. HOOP OR FARMER-STYLE COTTAGE CHEESE

1 CAN MUSHROOM STEMS AND PIECES   ½ C. PARSLEY, CHOPPED

1/3 C. MILK   2 C. COOKED BROWN RICE

1 TSP SALT

COMBINE ONION AND MUSHROOMS; ADD CHEESE, PARSLEY, MILK AND SALT. MIX THOROUGHLY AND BAKE IN GREASED CASSEROLE IN 350 DEGREES OVEN, 14 MINUTES.

CHEESE-STUFFED APPLES

½ C. HOOP CHEESE OR FARMER-STYLE COTTAGE CHEESE   4 APPLES, CORED

¼ C. LEMON OR PINEAPPLE JUICE   1/3 C. CHOPPED DATES OR RAISINS

MIX CHEESE WITH DATES OR RAISINS; MIX AND STUFF INTO CENTERS OF CORED APPLES. IF APPLES HAVE BEEN SPRAYED WITH A POISON SPRAY, THEY SHOULD BE

PEELED. CUT APPLES IN SLICES, SPRINKLE WITH LEMON OR PINEAPPLE, SPRINKLE WITH LEMON OR PINEAPPLE JUICE AND SERVE ON CRISP LETTUCE LEAVES.

SQUASH-CHEESE CASSEROLE

6 MEDIUM ZUCCHINI OR SUMMER SQUASH   1 TSP SALT

1 EGG, BEATEN   DASH OF TABASCO

¼ C. WHOLE WHEAT CRUMBS   ½ C. BUTTERED WHOLE WHEAT CRUMBS

½ C. HOOP CHEESE   ¼ TSP MARJORAM

1 TSP PAPRIKA

COOK SQUASH OR ZUCCHINI IN BOILING WATER UNTIL TENDER. CUT IN SMALL PIECES; BLEND WITH EGG, ¼ C. CRUMBS, CHEESE AND SEASONINGS. POUR INTO GREASED CASSEROLE; TOP WITH CRUMBS, SPRINKLE WITH PAPRIKA. BAKE AT 350 DEGREES, 20 MINUTES.

MEATLESS CHILI WITH CHEESE

2 TSP MINCED ONION OR 1 TBSP DRY ONION SOUP MIX   ½ C. MILK

1 TBSP SALAD OIL   3 TSP CHILI POWDER

1 5OZ. CAN TOMATO SAUCE   1 C. FRESHLY-GRATED CHEESE

2 BEATEN EGGS

BROWN MINCED ONION OR DRY SOUP MIX IN SALAD OIL. ADD TOMATO SAUCE, MILK, CHILI POWDER. SIMMER, BUT DO NOT BOIL, FOR 15 MINUTES. ADD CHEESE, EGGS, AND SEASON TO TASTE. SERVE ON TOAST.

CHEESE CROQUETTES

1 C. DRIED WHOLE GRAIN BREAD CRUMBS   DASH OF TABASCO

2 C. GRATED PARMESAN OR SHARP CHEDDAR CHEESE   1 EGG, WELL BEATEN

1 TSP PREPARED MUSTARD   2 TBSP TOP MILK

DRIED BREAD CRUMBS	1/8 TSP BLACK PEPPER

SOFTEN CRUMBS WITH ENOUGH WATER TO SHAPE. MIX WITH GRATED CHEESE, MUSTARD, SALT, PEPPER, TABASCO, EGG AND MILK. SHAPE INTO 6-8 CONICAL CROQUETTES, ROLL IN ADDITIONAL DRIED BREAD CRUMBS. FRY IN DEEP HOT OIL, OR BAKE AT 350 DEGREES, TURNING OFTEN. DRAIN ON BROWN PAPER AND SERVE WITH TOMATO SAUCE.

CHEESE SAUCE

4 TBSP BUTTER OR OIL	¼ TSP NUTMEG
4 TBSP FLOUR	1 TBSP GRATED ONION
¼ TSP PEPPER	2 C. MILK
½ TSP SALT	1 C. GRATED CHEDDAR CHEESE

MELT BUTTER IN MEDIUM-SIZE SAUCEPAN. BLEND IN FLOUR, ONION, SALT, PEPPER AND NUTMEG. SLOWLY STIR IN MILK. COOK OVER LOW HEAT, STIRRING CONSTANTLY UNTIL SAUCE THICKENS AND BOILS, ABOUT 1 MINUTE. ADD GRATED CHEESE. CONTINUE TO COOK OVER LOW HEAT, STIRRING CONSTANTLY UNTIL CHEESE MELTS. SERVE OVER BAKED POTATO, MACARONI, BROCCOLI OR SALMON CROQUETTES. MAKES 2 CUPS.

CHEESE THINS

2 C. SHARP CHEDDAR CHEESE, GRATED	½ C. BUTTER

1 GREEN PEPPER, MINCED FINE OR ½ C. MINCED SWEET RED PEPPER, OR ½ C. CHOPPED CANNED PIMENTO

2 C. UNBLEACHED WHITE FLOUR

CREAM CHEESE AND BUTTER THOROUGHLY. ADD FLOUR GRADUALLY AND ADD PEPPER OR PIMENTO. SHAPE INTO A ROLL. WRAP IN PARCHMENT PAPER OR OILED PAPER. CHILL IN REFRIGERATOR SEVERAL HOURS. JUST BEFORE SERVING, SLICE AND BAKE ON COOKIE SHEET, AT 400 DEGREES, UNTIL LIGHTLY BROWNED.

CHEESEBURGERS, MEATLESS

2 8OZ. PACKAGES COTTAGE CHEESE	1 TBSP MINCED PARSLEY
1 BEATEN EGG	¾ TSP SALT
¾ C WHOLE WHEAT BREAD CRUMBS	1 TSP WORCESTERSHIRE SAUCE
2 TBSP MINCED ONION	1 C. FINE BREAD CRUMBS

COMBINE COTTAGE CHEESE WITH EGG, BREAD CRUMBS, ONION, PARSLEY, SALT AND WORCESTERSHIRE SAUCE. FORM INTO 6-8 CAKES AND COAT WITH FINE BREAD CRUMBS. FRY IN BUTTER OR OIL UNTIL BROWN ON BOTH SIDES. SERVE WITH BOTTLED CHILI SAUCE.

OLIVE- CHEESE TURNOVERS

PASTRY ROUNDS	1/3 C. CHILI SAUCE
2/3 C. GRATED CHEDDAR CHEESE	CHILI POWDER TO TASTE
2/3 C. CHOPPED RIPE OLIVES	CUMIN POWDER

PREPARE 1 RECIPE OF YOUR FAVORITE PASTRY, ROLL INTO 2-INCH ROUNDS. MIX GRATED CHEESE WITH OLIVES, CHILI SAUCE, CHILI POWDER AND DASH OF CUMIN. PLACE 1 TSP OF FILLING ON EACH PASTRY ROUND, MOISTEN EDGES, FOLD OVER HALF AND PINCH EDGES TOGETHER. PLACE ON COOKIE SHEET. CHILL. WHEN READY TO SERVE, BAKE 10-12 MINUTES, AT 475 DEGREES. SERVE HOT, AS HORS D'OEUVRES.

CREAM CHEESE SAVOURIES

START THESE THE DAY BEFORE FOR BEST RESULTS.

½ LB FLOUR	¼ LB BUTTER OR MARGARINE
A PINCH OF SALT	¼ LB CREAM CHEESE

SIFT THE FLOUR, ADD SALT AND USING A KNIFE, ADD THE CREAM CHEESE AND BUTTER, CUTTING IT INTO SMALL PIECES. MAKE INTO A DOUGH AND THEN WRAP

IT IN GREASEPROOF PAPER AND LEAVE IT IN THE REFRIGERATOR OVERNIGHT. ROLL IT OUT NEXT DAY ON THE PAPER ORTIL IT IS AS THIN AS A PENNY AND THEN CUT INTO SHAPES OR ROUNDS. BAKE IN A HOT OVEN (400 DEGREES) FOR 10-15 MINUTES. SERVE VERY HOT.

CHEESE AND OLIVES ON TOAST

2 SLICES OF CHEESE PER PERSON   PREPARED MUSTARD AS REQUIRED

12 OLIVES   SLICES OF DARK BROWN BREAD AS REQUIRED

1 CAN ASPARAGUS TIPS

BEGIN BY TOASTING THE BREAD ON ONE SIDE AND SPREADING THE OTHER WITH THE MUSTARD. ALLOW 2 SLICES OF BREAD PER SERVING. CHOP THE OLIVES AND PLACE ON TOP OF THE MUSTARD. COVER WITH THE CHEESE SLICES AND BROWN GENTLY UNDER THE GRILL. GARNISH WITH PARSLEY AND CHOPPED CHIVES.

PEPPERS WITH CHEESE

6 LARGE GREEN OR RED PEPPERS   ¾ C. COTTAGE CHEESE

3 MEDIUM EGGS   PAPRIKA

2 TBSP BUTTER   SALT TO TASTE

WASH THE PEPPERS AND REMOVE SEEDS AND PITH. SHRED THEM FINELY AND FRY THEM IN THE BUTTER FOR 2 MINUTES. SEASON WITH SALT. PLACE IN A CASSEROLE, ADD A LAYER OF CHEESE, THEN THE BEATEN EGGS SPRINKLE WITH PLENTY OF PAPRIKA AND BAKE FOR 15 MINUTES AT 325 DEGREES.

SOBER WELSH RAREBIT

2 C. GRATED SHARP CHEESE   4 TBSP MILK

2 TBSP BUTTER   1 TSP MUSTARD

HOT BUTTERED TOAST   PARSLEY

MELT THE BUTTER IN A SMALL SAUCEPAN, ADD THE CHEESE, MILK, MUSTARD AND PEPPER AND COOK OVER A VERY GENTLE HEAT UNTIL THE MIXTURE IS SMOOTH. TASTE TO SEE IF SALT IS NEEDED. PUT ON TOP OF HOT BUTTERED TOAST AND PUT UNDER THE GRILL UNTIL THE MIXTURE IS BROWN AND BUBBLY. GARNISH WITH SPRIGS OF PARSLEY.

EGGS

COOKING EGGS:
HIGH HEAT TOUGHENS EGGS. A DELICATE, TENDER, WELL-COOKED EGG CAN BE PRODUCED ONLY IF YOU COOK IT AT A LOW HEAT.

SOFT-COOKED (BOILED) EGGS:
EGGS COOKED IN THE SHELL ARE STILL GENERALLY CALLED "BOILED EGGS", EITHER SOFT-BOILED OR HARD-BOILED. PROPERLY SPEAKING, HOWEVER, EGGS SHOULD NEVER BE BOILED, ONLY SIMMERED. THE WATER SHOULD COMPLETELY COVER THE EGGS AND SHOULD NOT BOIL ONCE THE EGGS HAVE BEEN PUT INTO IT.

BRING WATER TO A BOIL IN A SAUCEPAN LARGE ENOUGH TO ACCOMMODATE THE NUMBER OF EGGS YOU PLAN TO COOK. LOWER THE EGGS CAREFULLY INTO THE WATER ON A SPOON AND REDUCE THE HEAT SO THAT THE WATER DOESN'T BUBBLE. LET THE WATER SIMMER 3-5 MINUTES, ACCORDING TO HOW HARD YOU LIKE YOUR EGGS. REMOVE THEM IMMEDIATELY WHEN THE TIME IS UP.

IT IS BEST TO LET THE EGGS STAND AT ROOM TEMPERATURE FOR A LITTLE WHILE BEFORE COOKING THEM. YOUR TIMING WILL BE MORE ACCURATE AND YOU RUN LESS RISK OF HAVING THE SHELLS CRACK WHEN THE HOT WATER TOUCHES THEM.

HARD-COOKED (BOILED) EGGS:
SIMMER THE EGGS IN WATER TO COVER AS DESCRIBED ABOVE, ALLOWING 15-20 MINUTES. STIR THE EGGS CAREFULLY WITH A SPOON ONCE OR TWICE DURING COOKING TO KEEP THE YOLK IN THE CENTER. TOO-HOT WATER OR TOO-LONG COOKING MAY GIVE THAT UNATTRACTIVE GREENISH RIM YOU SOMETIMES SEE AROUND THE YOLK OF A HARD-BOILED EGG.

EGGS A LA MODE:
BUTTER GENEROUSLY A SLICE OF WHOLE WHEAT TOAST FOR EACH PERSON TO BE SERVED. ON IT PLACE ONE OR TWO HOT SOFT-COOKED EGGS REMOVED FROM THE SHELL WITHOUT BREAKING. COVER EACH PORTION WITH 1/3 C. OF WELL-SEASONED HOT STEWED TOMATOES. SERVE ON A HOT PLATTER AND GARNISH EACH WITH A SPRIG OF FRESH WATERCRESS OR PARSLEY. MORE TOMATO MAY BE SERVED FROM A SEPARATE DISH IF DESIRED.

POACHED EGGS: IF THE EGGS ARE NOT PERFECTLY FRESH, PICK SOME OTHER WAY OF COOKING THEM. POACHING, FOR GOOD RESULTS, DEMANDS A PERFECTLY FRESH EGG.

FILL A SHALLOW PAN OR SKILLET TWO-THIRDS FULL OF WATER. ADD ½ TSP OF VEGETABLE SALT FOR EACH 2 C. OF HOT WATER. BRING THE WATER TO THE BOIL AND REDUCE THE HEAT. BREAK EACH EGG INTO A CUP AND SLIP IT INTO THE WATER. DON'T TRY TO COOK MORE EGGS THAN CAN SIT COMFORTABLY IN THE WATER WITHOUT TOUCHING EACH OTHER. WHEN ALL THE EGGS ARE IN THE WATER, COVER THE PAN AND SIMMER GENTLY FOR 3-5 MINUTES: LONGER IF YOU LIKE THE YOLK FIRM. LIFT THE EGGS FROM THE WATER WITH A DRAINING SPOON AND SERVE IMMEDIATELY ON BUTTERED WHOLE WHEAT TOAST.

SHIRRED EGGS: BUTTER A SHIRRING DISH FOR EACH PERSON TO BE SERVED. IN EACH DISH PUT 1 TSP RAW CELERY JUICE (OR ANY OTHER DESIRED VEGETABLE JUICE) AND 1 TBSP OF HEAVY CREAM. BREAK AN EGG INTO EACH DISH AND SPRINKLE WITH VEGETABLE SALT. SET THE DISHES INTO A PAN OF HOT WATER AND BAKE IN A MODERATE OVEN (350 DEGREES) UNTIL THE EGG IS SUFFICIENTLY SET ABOUT 10 MINUTES. GARNISH WITH CHOPPED PARSLEY OR PAPRIKA.

SCRAMBLED EGGS: BREAK FRESH EGGS IN A BOWL. ADD A GENEROUS TABLE SPOONFUL OF CREAM FOR EACH EGG, AND SPRINKLE WITH VEGETABLE SALT TO TASTE. BEAT UNTIL BLENDED WITH A ROTARY EGG BEATER. MELT BUTTER IN A HEAVY SKILLET AND POUR IN THE EGGS. COOK OVER LOW HEAT, STIRRING UP COOKED LAYER OF EGG ALONG THE BOTTOM OF THE PAN AS IT FORMS. WHEN THE EGGS ARE DONE, EITHER FIRM OR A LITTLE WET AS YOUR TASTE REQUIRES, REMOVE IMMEDIATELY FROM HEAT AND FROM THE SKILLET AND SERVE.

BEFORE COOKING THE EGG MIXTURE, YOU CAN ADD GRATED ONION, FINELY CHOPPED CHIVES, MINCED PARSLEY OR SAUTEED CHOPPED FRESH MUSHROOMS.

FRENCH OMELET: FRENCH OMELET IS MADE WITH THE SAME MIXTURE AS SCRAMBLED EGGS. THE DIFFERENCE IS IN THE WAY OF COOKING. INSTEAD OF STIRRING UP THE EGGS AS THEY COOK, LIFT THE EDGE OF THE BOTTOM GENTLY WITH A SPATULA AND TIP THE SKILLET TO LET THE UNCOOKED TOP RUN UNDER

THE BOTTOM AND BE COOKED IN ITS TURN. WHEN THE BOTTOM IS BROWN AND THE OMELET IS FIRM ALL THROUGH, FOLD IT IN HALF AND SERVE. CHEESE, VEGETABLES, CHOPPED LEFTOVER MEAT OR CHICKEN CAN BE SPREAD OVER THE TOP OF THE OMELET BEFORE YOU FOLD IT.

APPLE OMELET

4 EGGS, WELL BEATEN	2 TBSP THICK CREAM
1 C. SHREDDED RAW APPLE	½ TSP VEGETABLE SALT
¼ C. TOMATO JUICE	

BEAT THE EGGS UNTIL LIGHT, THEN BEAT IN THE OTHER INGREDIENTS. POUR INTO A WELL-OILED BAKING DISH AND BAKE IN A MODERATE OVEN (375 DEGREES) ABOUT 15 MINUTES, UNTIL BROWNED.

EGG OMELET WITH SQUASH

2 EGGS	½ GREEN PEPPER, COARSELY CHOPPED
2 TBSP VEGETABLE OIL	3/8 TSP VEGETABLE SALT
2 C. CUBED SUMMER SQUASH	2 TBSP VEGETABLE OIL OR BUTTER
1½ C. CUBED TOMATO	

SOFT-COOK THE EGGS. WHILE THEY ARE COOKING, HEAT THE VEGETABLE OIL IN A COVERED CASSEROLE OR SKILLET. ADD THE PREPARED VEGETABLES AND STEW SLOWLY UNTIL THE SQUASH IS SUFFICIENTLY TENDER--ABOUT 15 MINUTES. ADD THE VEGETABLE SALT. SHELL AND CHOP THE EGGS AND ADD TO THE VEGETABLE MIXTURE. GARNISH WITH A SPRINKLING OF CHOPPED CHIVES.

RAGOUT OF EGGS

1/3 C. VEGETABLE OIL	1 LARGE RIPE TOMATO
1 ONION, CHOPPED	1/8 TSP POWDERED SAGE
½ EGGPLANT, CUBED	3/8 TSP VEGETABLE SALT

½ CLOVE GARLIC, MINCED   3 HARD-COOKED EGGS CUT IN 16THS

½ PIMENTO, DICED   3 TBSP MINCED PARSLEY

PUT HALF OF THE OIL IN A HEAVY SKILLET AND BROWN THE ONION AND EGGPLANT IN IT. ADD THE REST OF THE OIL, THE OTHER VEGETABLES, AND THE SAGE. COVER AND SIMMER GENTLY ABOUT 10 MINUTES, UNTIL THE EGGPLANT IS COOKED THROUGH. ADD THE SALT, THE PIECES OF EGG AND HEAT THE EGGS THROUGH. STIR IN THE PARSLEY JUST BEFORE DISHING UP. SERVE WITH TOAST POINTS.

EGG CHOP SUEY

3 TBSP VEGETABLE OIL   1 LARGE GREEN PEPPER CUT IN SQUARES

2 MEDIUM ONIONS CUT IN THIN WEDGES

1 4-EGG OMELET, WELL BROWNED ON BOTH SIDES AND CUT INTO CUBES

5 LARGE STALKS OF CELERY CUT IN 1-INCH PIECES

2/3 CAN TOMATO SOUP   ½ TSP VEGETABLE SALT

HEAT THE OIL IN A COVERED SKILLET. SAUTE THE ONION AND CELERY IN THE OIL FOR 15-20 MINUTES, ADDING A LITTLE WATER IF NECESSARY TO KEEP THEM FROM BURNING. FIVE MINUTES BEFORE THEY ARE SOFT, ADD THE GREEN PEPPER. AND WHEN THE VEGETABLES ARE DONE, ADD THE OMELET AND TOMATO SOUP AND VEGETABLE SALT. STIR OVER LOW HEAT UNTIL HEATED THROUGH. SERVE IN A RING OF HOT MASHED SUMMER SQUASH OR OTHER COOKED VEGETABLE, WELL SEASONED.

CHINESE EGGS

3 EGGS   ¾ TBSP BUTTER AND VEGETABLE OIL MIXED

1½ C. SHREDDED RAW VEGETABLES ¾ TSP VEGETABLE SALT

BEAT THE EGGS AND SHREDDED VEGETABLES TOGETHER UNTIL THE MIXTURE IS THICK. MAKE SURE THE EGG IS EVENLY DISTRIBUTED THROUGH THE VEGETABLES.

TAKE A THIRD OF THE MIXTURE AND PRESS AGAINST THE CURVING SIDES OF A TEACUP OR LADLE SO THAT THE VEGETABLES WILL LIE FLAT WHEN THE MIXTURE IS CAREFULLY POURED INTO THE FRYING PAN. HEAT THE FAT IN THE SKILLET AND POUR IN THE MIXTURE TO MAKE 3 THIN FLAT CAKES. BROWN ON ONE SIDE, SALT, AND TURN OVER, THEN BROWN THE OTHER SIDE--ABOUT 10 MINUTES IN ALL.

ANY QUICK-COOKING TENDER VEGETABLES MAY BE USED ALONE OR IN COMBINATION. ONE PART CUCUMBER TO 2 PARTS SPINACH IS GOOD; OR SUMMER SQUASH OR EGGPLANT AND ONION WITH GREEN PEPPER, OR A MIXTURE OF LEAFY GREENS.

EGGS ON VEGETABLE TOAST

FOR EACH PERSON TO BE SERVED, CUT A SLICE OF EGGPLANT ¾ INCH THICK. MOISTEN IN MILK OR EGG DILUTED WITH MILK AND DUST WITH WHOLE WHEAT FLOUR. PLACE IN A BUTTERED BAKING DISH, ALLOWING 1 TBSP OF BUTTER FOR EACH SLICE. BAKE IN A HOT OVEN (400 DEGREES) UNTIL THE BOTTOM IS BROWNED, ABOUT 15 MINUTES. TURN THE SLICES OVER AND IN THE CENTER OF EACH SCOOP OUT A HOLLOW LARGE ENOUGH TO HOLD AN EGG YOLK. SPRINKLE WITH VEGETABLE SALT AND BREAK AN EGG INTO EACH HOLLOW. RETURN TO THE OVEN AND BAKE UNTIL THE EGG IS SET--ABOUT 5 MINUTES. SPRINKLE WITH PAPRIKA AND SERVE WITH A GARNISH OF ANY DESIRED GREEN.

POACHED EGGS DE LUXE

SEPARATE EACH EGG, BEING CAREFUL NOT TO BREAK THE YOLK. BEAT EACH WHITE SEPARATELY UNTIL STIFF AND SLIDE INTO BUTTERED RAMEKIN OR WELL OF MUFFIN TIN. PLACE YOLK IN CENTER AND POACH IN SHALLOW PAN OF HOT WATER. DOT WITH BUTTER, SPRINKLE WITH SALT AND PEPPER AND SERVE WITH TRIANGLES OF BUTTERED WHOLE WHEAT TOAST.

OMELET SOUFFLE (BASIC RECIPE)

4 EGGS, SEPARATED	½ TSP PEPPER
4 TBSP MILK	1 TBSP BUTTER

1 TSP SALT

BEAT EGG WHITES UNTIL THEY STAND IN PEAKS. BEAT YOLKS LIGHTLY AND BLEND WITH MILK. ADD SALT AND PEPPER. FOLD IN EGG WHITES. MELT BUTTER IN SKILLET OVER THE LOW HEAT. POUR IN OMELET MIXTURE, WHICH SHOULD BE ABOUT 2-INCHES DEEP IN PAN. CONTINUE COOKING OVER LOW HEAT ON TOP OF STOVE, MEANWHILE PRE-HEATING OVEN TO 325 DEGREES. WHEN BOTTOM OF OMELET IS LIGHT BROWN, REMOVE FROM TOP OF STOVE AND BAKE IN OVEN ABOUT 8 MINUTES, OR UNTIL KNIFE BLADE INSERTED IN OMELET COMES OUT CLEAN. SLIDE ONTO PLATTER AND FOLD IN HALF.

VARIATIONS: USE ANY OF THE FOLLOWING AS FILLING FOR OMELET, PLACING ON HALF THE OMELET JUST BEFORE FOLDING IT OVER:

1. HEAVY CREAM AND PIECES OF BUTTER
2. SAUTEED CHOPPED TOMATOES
3. CRUMBLED CRISP BACON (BEEF)
4. MINCED ONIONS COOKED IN BUTTER UNTIL TENDER, BUT NOT BROWN
5. CHOPPED, COOKED MUSHROOMS
6. COTTAGE CHEESE
7. CHOPPED STUFFED OLIVES
8. AVOCADO CUBES MARINATED IN LEMON JUICE
9. MINCED SUNFLOWER SEED SPROUTS
10. GRATED CHEDDAR OR SWISS CHEESE
11. CHOPPED GREEN ONIONS AND TOPS, AND CHOPPED GREEN PEPPERS.

EGGS FLORENTINE

LINE INDIVIDUAL BUTTERED CASSEROLES WITH HOT, CREAMED SPINACH. ADD 2 CAREFULLY POACHED EGGS TO EACH AND POUR OVER EACH CASSEROLE A RICH WHITE ONION SAUCE. TOP WITH GRATED PARMESAN CHEESE AND BROWN UNDER BROILER.

EGGS AND RICE CASSEROLE

| 1 CUP RICE | 2 CUPS WATER | 1/8 TEAS CINNAMON |

¼ CUP GREEN PEPPER	SALT AND PEPPER	¼ CUP DRY ONION
¾ STICK BUTTER	2 EGGS	1 TAB. TOMATO PASTE

BROWN RICE IN PART OF BUTTER, ADD WATER AND COOK UNTIL TENDER. BROWN ONION AND PEPPER IN BUTTER FOR 10 MIN. ADD TO COOKED RICE. BEAT EGGS, COOK IN BUTTER UNTIL SET, ADD TO RICE AND BLEND, ADD A LITTLE WATER IF NEEDED, COVER POT AND STEAM FOR ABOUT 10 MIN. SERVE WITH ANY MEAT.

CHOPPED OKRA

1½ LB OKRA	2 CLOVES GARLIC	½ STICK BUTTER
2 MED ONIONS	2 TAB. TOMATO PASTE	SALT AND PEPPER
1 GREEN PEPPER	2 TAB. WATER	¼ TEAS. LAWRY SALT
1 TAB. FLOUR		

CLEAN AND CUT OKRA IN ABOUT HALF INCH PIECES, SEASON WITH SALT AND PEPPER AND FLOUR. MELT HALF OF BUTTER IN SKILLET, ADD OKRA AND COOK ON A LOW FLAME UNTIL TENDER, STIRRING OFTEN TO KEEP FROM BROWNING, IN ANOTHER SKILLET AND REST OF BUTTER AND VEGETABLES, BROWN SLIGHTLY, COVER AND STEAM TENDER. THEN ADD PASTE AND WATER COOK FOR ABOUT FIVE MIN. POUR OVER OKRA, COVER AND STEAM ON LOW FLAME FOR 10 MIN.

CAULIFLOWER (EGYPTIAN STYLE)

1 MED. CAULIFLOWER	2 TEAS. SALT	½ STICK BUTTER
2 WHOLE EGGS	½ STICK BUTTER	2 MED. ONIONS

SEPARATE AND CLEAN BUDS, DROP IN BOILING SALTED WATER FOR 5 MIN. REMOVE FROM WATER, CHOP ONIONS AND BROWN IN BUTTER. ADD TOMATO PASTE TO BROWNED ONIONS, BEAT EGGS, DIP THE CAULIFLOWER IN THE BEATEN EGGS AND BROWN IN BUTTER SLIGHTLY. POUR TOMATO PASTE AND ONIONS OVER THE CAULIFLOWER. COVER AND STEAM IN 350 DEGREES FOR 20 MIN.

CAULIFLOWER NO. 1

1 MED. CAULIFLOWER	1 TEAS. SALT	FEW DASHES PAPRIKA

½ GREEN PEPPER   2 TAB. MAZOLA OIL   2 TAB. BUTTER

SEPARATE BUDS AND CLEAN. PLACE IN POT UPRIGHT, STEAM PART DOWN, SPRINKLE SALT AND PAPRIKA OVER TOP, LAY GREEN PEPPER IN THIS. POUR BUTTER AND OIL OVER. DO NOT ADD WATER. COVER TIGHTLY AND STEAM UNTIL TENDER, BE CAREFUL NOT TO OVERCOOK.

CAULIFLOWER NO. 2

1 MED. CAULIFLOWER	½ CUP WATER	¼ CUP BROWN SUGAR
½ TEAS. SALT	¼ TEAS. GARLIC SALT	½ CUP TOASTED CRUMBS
½ STICK BUTTER	½ GREEN PEPPER	

CLEAN AND BOIL IN SALTED WATER AND GREEN PEPPER FOR ABOUT FIVE MIN. REMOVE FROM WATER, PLACE IN DISH, MIX SUGAR, CRUMBS AND GARLIC SALT, SPRINKLE OVER IT. POUR OVER MELTED BUTTER, COVER, PLACE IN OVEN 350 DEG. FOR 20 TO 30 MIN. SERVE TWO TO FOUR.

BAKED STUFFED SUMMER SQUASH

2 LBS. SQUASH	1/8 TEAS. ACCENT	DASH OF CINNAMON
½ STICK BUTTER	½ LB MEAT	SALT AND PEPPER
2 CLOVES OF GARLIC	1/3 CUP TOASTED BREAD CRUMBS	1 GREEN PEPPER
2 TOMATOES	1 TAB. CHOP PARSLEY	3 MED. ONIONS
¼ TEAS. LAWRY SALT		

STEAM SQUASH FOR 10 MIN. ON BOTH SIDES IN A PAN OF WATER, REMOVE FROM WATER, SLICE OFF THE TOP AND REMOVE THE CENTER AND ALL SEEDS, BUT SAVE PULP. HOLLOW OUT SQUASH AND BRUSH THE INSIDES WITH BUTTER, SALT AND PEPPER. HEAT BUTTER IN SKILLET, ONIONS, PEPPER, PULP, GARLIC AND TOMATOES. COOK FOR 5 MIN., ADD MEAT, COOK AND STIR UNTIL IT BECOMES GRAINY, ADD CRUMBS AND PARSLEY AND SEASONINGS, BLEND WELL, FILL EACH SQUASH AND BAKE IN OVEN 350 DEGREES FOR 34 TO 40 MIN.

STUFFED ZUCCHINI SQUASH (PLAIN)

8 SMALL SQUASH	2 EGGS	½ CAN TOMATO PASTE

½ LB GROUND MEAT	1½ CUP WATER	1 GREEN PEPPER
½ TEAS. LAWRY SALT	2 MED ONIONS	½ STICK BUTTER
¼ TEAS. PAPRIKA	2 CLOVES GARLIC	SALT AND PEPPER

CHOP VEGETABLES, ADD TO GROUND MEAT, ADD BEATEN EGGS AND SEASONINGS. CLEAN SQUASH, CUT OFF STEM AND HOLLOW OUT SQUASH VERY CAREFULLY, DO NOT BREAK. FILL WITH MEAT MIXTURE, PLACE IN BAKING DISH OR ROASTER, POUR OVER MELTED BUTTER AND PASTE DILUTED WITH WATER, COVER AND COOK IN OVEN 350 DEGREES.

STUFFED CUCUMBERS (COMBINATION)

1 LB. MED TOMATOES	¼ TEAS. CINNAMON	½ LB. GROUND MEAT
4 LARGE ONIONS	¼ CUP BROWN RICE	1 GREEN PEPPER
2 MED. CUCUMBERS	½ CUP TOASTED CRUMBS	2 CLOVES GARLIC
½ STICK BUTTER	2 TAB. TOMATO PASTE	SALT AND PEPPER

PEEL ONIONS AND PLACE IT WHOLE IN A POT WITH ABOUT 2 CUPS OF BOILING WATER. LET IT BOIL FOR ABOUT 5 OR 8 MIN. OR UNTIL THE ONIONS BECOME TENDER. REMOVE FROM WATER, BUT SAVE THE WATER. LET ONIONS COOL ENOUGH FOR YOU TO HANDLE. TAKE A PARING KNIFE AND TAKE THE CENTER OUT, LEAVING ABOUT 3 OR 4 LAYERS OF THE ONIONS SECTIONS, CUT CUCUMBERS IN HALVES, THEN TAKE THE CENTERS OF ONIONS AND COOK IN BUTTER FOR 10 MIN. THEN ADD MEAT AND THE INSIDE OF THE TOMATOES AND CUCUMBERS AND COOK UNTIL THE MEAT BECOMES GRAINY, ADD SEASONINGS, RICE AND CRUMBS, BLEND WELL, FILL EACH VEGETABLE AND PLACE UPRIGHT IN ROASTER. POUR OVER PASTE DILUTED WITH SOME OF THE WATER FROM BOILING THE ONIONS, ADD SODA, COVER ROASTER AND COOK IN 400 DEGREES OVEN UNTIL DONE. SERVE 2 TO 4.

NO. 1 ASPARAGUS CASSEROLE

1 TEN OZ. CAN ASPARAGUS	½ GREEN PEPPER	½ LB. GROUND MEAT
2 MED. ONIONS	½ CUP TOASTED CRUMBS	(OR OMIT MEAT)
2 MED. TOMATOES	1 CLOVE OF GARLIC	SALT AND PEPPER

½ STICK BUTTER	1 TAB. CHOPPED PARSLEY	DASH OF CINNAMON

MELT BUTTER IN SKILLET ADD SLICED ONIONS, PEPPER AND GARLIC, COVER AND COOK ON A LOW FLAME UNTIL TENDER. DO NOT BROWN. ADD MEAT, STIR IT UNTIL IT BECOMES GRAINY, ADD SLICED TOMATOES AND SEASONINGS. COOK FOR 5 MIN. LINE BOTTOM OF DISH WITH CRUMBS. POUR ON SOME MEAT MIXTURE, THEN ADD ASPARAGUS, POUR THE REMAINING MEAT ON THE TOP WITH CRUMBS. BAKE IN OVEN 350 DEGREES FOR ABOUT 45 MIN. SERVE 2 TO 4.

NO. 2 ASPARAGUS CASSEROLE

2 CANS OR PACKAGES ASPARAGUS	1/8 TEAS. RED PEPPER	½ STICK BUTTER
3 WHOLE EGGS	¼ LB CHEESE	¼ TEAS. GARLIC SALT	1 TSP. SALT
2 CUPS MILK	1/8 TEAS. PEPPER	2 TAB. WATER	1/8 TEAS. PAPRIKA

SCALD MILK TO THE BOILING POINT, MELT CHEESE IN WATER. SLOWLY ADD MILK TO MELTED CHEESE SLOWLY STIRRING TO PREVENT LUMPING. BEAT EGGS ADD MILK AND CHEESE SLOWLY, BLEND WELL ADD SEASONINGS. PLACE COOKED ASPARAGUS IN CASSEROLE, POUR MIXTURE OVER AND PLACE IN A PAN OF WATER, PUT IN OVEN AND BAKE AT 350 DEGREES FOR ABOUT 40 MIN. SERVES 4 TO 6.

NO. 3 PLAIN ASPARAGUS

1 OR 2 BUNCHES ASPARAGUS	2 OR 3 TAB, BUTTER	SALT AND PEPPER
½ GREEN PEPPER	¼ CUP WATER	DASH OF PAPRIKA

CLEAN BY CUTTING OFF THE TOUGH END, AND WASH WELL. PLACE IN POT. ADD SEASONINGS. COVER THE POT TIGHTLY, COOK ON A LOW FLAME UNTIL TENDER, ADD MORE WATER IF NEEDED.

EGGPLANT AND RICE CASSEROLE

MEAT AND RICE CAN BE OMITTED. IF SO, THEN USE 1 CUP TOASTED BREAD CRUMBS AND 1 CUP TOMATOES OR TOMATO JUICE.

2 CUPS COOKED RICE	2 TAB. PARSLEY	1 LARGE EGGPLANT

2 MED. ONIONS	2 GARLIC CLOVES	2 TAB. GRATED CHEESE
2 TAB. TOMATO PASTE	1/8 TEAS. CINNAMON	1 STICK BUTTER

PEEL AND SLICE EGGPLANT, SPRINKLE ON SALT, LET SET FOR 10 MIN. DRAIN, CUT IN SMALL PIECES USE HALF OF BUTTER AND COOK UNTIL SOFT. MELT REST OF BUTTER IN SKILLET, ADD ONIONS, GARLIC AND MEAT, COOK (STIR CONTINUALLY UNTIL MEAT BECOMES GRAINY ON A LOW FLAME UNTIL ONIONS ARE TENDER.) ADD PASTE, PARSLEY AND SEASONINGS, TURN OFF FLAME, COVER SKILLET, STEAM FOR 5 MIN. ADD MEAT TO EGGPLANT, BLEND WELL. LINE BOTTOM OF BAKING DISH WITH RICE, POUR ON MIXTURE, COVER WITH REMAINING RICE, SPRINKLE TOP WITH CHEESE, COVER AND SIMMER IN OVEN 350 DEG. FOR 30 MIN. SERVE 4 TO 6.

BATTERED EGGPLANT

1 OR 2 EGGPLANTS (MED.)	¼ TEAS. PAPRIKA	½ STICK BUTTER
1 WHOLE EGG	1 CUP TOASTED CRUMBS	¼ CUP MAZOLA OIL
SALT	PEPPER	

WASH, PEEL AND SLICE IN MED. PIECES. BEAT EGG, DIP SLICES IN EGG THEN DIP IN CRUMBS, COAT IT WELL, SHAKE OFF EXCESS CRUMBS AND PLACE IN HOT BUTTER, EACH SLICE SEPARATELY. BROWN LIGHTLY ON MED. FLAME, REMOVE FROM SKILLET AND PLACE IN PAN, ADD SEASONINGS, COVER AND STEAM IN OVEN 350 DEGREES FOR 20 MIN.

ROASTED EGGPLANT

1 OR 2 EGGPLANTS (MED)	½ GREEN PEPPER	SALT & PEPPER
2 OR 3 MED. ONIONS	½ TEAS. PAPRIKA	½ STICK BUTTER
2 TAB. TOMATO PASTE	1/8 TEAS. CINNAMON	

WASH, PEEL AND SLICE EGGPLANT IN THICK PIECES. SLICE ONIONS AND PEPPER TO FINE PIECES, MELT BUTTER IN ROASTER, ADD VEGETABLES AND SEASONINGS, COVER THE ROASTER, BAKE IN OVEN 350 DEGREES UNTIL DONE.

STRING BEANS

1 LB. BEANS	½ GREEN PEPPER	1/8 TEAS. BLACK PEPPER
¼ CUP OIL	½ TEAS. SALT	DASH OF TURMERIC
1/8 TEAS. PAPRIKA	1 MED. ONION	1 CLOVE OF GARLIC

CLEAN AND CUT IN MED. PIECES, WASH, PUT IN POT AND ADD SEASONINGS. DO NOT ADD WATER AT THIS POINT. COVER AND COOK ON A LOW FLAME FOR 45 MINS. THEN ADD LITTLE WATER IF NEEDED AND COOK UNTIL BEANS ARE DONE. SERVE 2 TO 4.

STRING BEANS (EGYPTIAN STYLE)

2 LBS. BEANS	1 STICK BUTTER	1 TEAS. SALT
1 CAN TOMATO PASTE	½ LB. GROUND BEEF	2 OR 3 ONIONS
PEPPER	1 CLOVE GARLIC	

CUT ONIONS FINE, COOK IN BUTTER UNTIL YELLOW, ADD MEAT, COOK AND STIR UNTIL ONIONS ARE LIGHT BROWN, THEN ADD TOMATO PASTE, COOK UNTIL THE MIXTURE IS DARK RED. CUT BEANS IN PIECES, ADD TO MIXTURE, MIX WELL. COVER BEANS WITH WATER, COOK UNTIL DONE, ADD MORE WATER IF NEEDED. WHEN BEANS ARE DONE LOWER THE FLAME AND SIMMER FOR 10 MIN. SERVE 4 TO 6.

GREEN PEAS WITH SAUCE

1 CAN OR PACKAGE OF PEAS	½ GREEN PEPPER	¼ CUP BREAD CRUMBS
1 LARGE ONION	2 LARGE TOMATOES	TOASTED
1 GARLIC CLOVE	1/8 TEAS. CINNAMON	¼ TEAS. LAWRY SALT
½ STICK BUTTER	STOCK OF PEAS OR WATER	SALT & PEPPER

HEAT BUTTER IN SKILLET, ADD CHOPPED ONION, PEPPER AND GARLIC. COOK TO A LIGHT BROWN, ADD TOMATO, STOCK, TOASTED CRUMBS AND SEASONINGS, BLEND WELL. ADD PEAS AND SEASONINGS, SIMMER ON A LOW FLAME FOR 30 MIN. SERVE 2 TO 6.

GREEN PEAS WITH POTATOES

2 OR 3 CUPS PEAS (FRESH)	½ STICK BUTTER	2 MED. POTATOES
½ CUP WATER	SALT & PEPPER	½ GREEN PEPPER
¼ CUP OIL (MAZOLA)	LITTLE PAPRIKA	

REMOVE PEAS FROM SHELL, WASH, PUT IN POT, ADD ALL INGREDIENTS EXCEPT POTATOES. LET COOK UNTIL PARTLY DONE, THEN ADD DICED POTATOES, CONTINUE TO COOK UNTIL ALL IS DONE. SERVE 4.

BAKED ZUCCHINI WITH CHEESE

1½ OR 2 LBS SQUASH	2 MED. ONIONS	CINNAMON
1 CUP TOMATOES	3 TAB. GRATED CHEESE	PEPPER
1 CUP TOASTED CRUMBS	2 TAB. CHOP PARSLEY	1 LB GROUND MEAT
½ STICK BUTTER	SALT	

BOIL SQUASH IN WATER FOR 5 MIN., REMOVE FROM WATER AND CUT IN HALVES, TAKE OUT THE PULP. MELT BUTTER IN SKILLET, ADD ONIONS, COOK FOR 5 MIN. ADD MEAT, PULP, TOMATOES, CRUMBS, PARSLEY AND SEASONING, BLEND WELL. COOK MIXTURE FOR 10 MIN. ARRANGE SQUASH IN BAKING DISH, FILL EACH WITH MIXTURE AND SPRINKLE CHEESE ON TOP, SPREAD REMAINING MIXTURE OVER ENTIRE DISH, BRUSH TOP WITH BUTTER, BAKE IN OVEN 350 DEGREES FOR 45 MIN. SERVE 4 TO 6.

SUMMER SQUASH (WHITE, YELLOW OR GREEN)

1 OR 2 LBS. SQUASH	1 TAB. CHOP PARSLEY	¼ TEAS. BLACK PEPPER
4 MED. ONIONS	½ TEAS. SALT	1 TO 2 TAB. OIL
FEW DASHES PAPRIKA	FEW DASHES TURMERIC	

CLEAN AND CUT IN MED PIECES. (RINSE THE VERY TENDER SQUASH). MELT BUTTER IN SKILLET AND ADD SQUASH, CHOPPED PARSLEY, ONIONS AND SEASONING. DO NOT ADD WATER. COVER SKILLET TIGHTLY AND STEAM ON LOW FLAME UNTIL WELL DONE. STIR TO PREVENT BURNING. SERVE 4 TO 6.

ZUCCHINI STUFFED SQUASH, ARABIC STYLE

½ LB. GROUND MEAT	1½ OR 2 LBS. SQUASH	1 GARLIC CLOVE
1 TAB. CHOP PARSLEY	3 MED. ONIONS	¼ TEAS. BLACK PEPPER
½ CUP RICE OR TOASTED CRUMBS	1/8 TEAS. CINNAMON	½ STICK BUTTER
	½ CAN TOMATO PASTE	½ GREEN PEPPER
2 CUPS WATER	SALT	(THE VERY SMALL SQUASH)

CLEAN AND CUT OFF THE STEM AND END OF SQUASH, HOLLOW OUT THE INSIDE, BE CAREFUL NOT TO CUT THROUGH THE OUTSIDE. BROWN AND PARTLY COOK RICE, MELT BUTTER IN SKILLET, ADD CHOPPED ONIONS, PEPPER, GARLIC, AND BROWN SLIGHTLY. ADD MEAT, THE INSIDE FROM SQUASH, RICE OR BREAD CRUMBS. CHOP PARSLEY AND SEASONINGS, BLEND WELL, COOK FOR 5 MINUTES. TAKE MIXTURE AND STUFF EACH SQUASH, PLACE UPRIGHT IN ROASTER, MIX PASTE WITH WATER, POUR OVER SQUASH UNTIL WELL DONE. ADD MORE WATER IF NEEDED. SERVE 4 TO 6.

STUFFED CABBAGE

1 LARGE WHITE CABBAGE	2 CUPS WATER	½ CUP OIL
1 GREEN PEPPER	¼ TEAS. ACCENT	2 CLOVES GARLIC
3 MED. ONIONS	¼ TEAS. CINN.	½ LB. GROUND OR CHOP MT.
½ CAN TOMATO PASTE	½ CUP BROWN RICE OR TOASTED CRUMBS	SALT & PEPPER

SEPARATE LEAVES OR PUT THE WHOLE HEAD OF CABBAGE IN WATER AND BOIL FOR ABOUT 5 MINUTES. HEAT OIL IN SKILLET; ADD MEAT, ONIONS, PEPPER, GARLIC AND COOK UNTIL ONIONS ARE TENDER. ADD SEASONINGS AND PARTLY COOKED RICE, BLEND. TAKE A LEAF OF CABBAGE , PUT IN LITTLE OF THE MEAT MIXTURE INTO IT AND FOLD IN THE SIDES AND ROLL IT. PLACE IT INTO ROASTER WITH OVERLAP ENDS DOWN. IF YOU GAVE MORE THAN 1 LAYER PLACE THE NEXT LAYER ACROSS-WISE, THEN POUR OVER CABBAGE TOMATO PASTE MIX WITH WATER TO COVER. PLACE A HEAVY PLATE ON TOP OF CABBAGES TO HOLD IN PLACE. COVER ROASTER AND COOK IN OVEN 400 DEGREES UNTIL DONE. SERVE 2 TO 4.

STUFFED PEPPERS

USE SAME INGREDIENTS AS FOR CABBAGES AND 6 TO 8 PEPPERS DEPENDING ON THE SIZE. TAKE STEM AND SEEDS OUT OF PEPPERS, BE CAREFUL NOT TO CRACK, FILL PEPPERS WITH MIXTURES AND PLACE IN ROASTER UPRIGHT. POUR TOMATO PASTE DILUTED WITH WATER TO HALF COVER INGREDIENTS, COVER ROASTER, COOK IN OVEN 400 DEGREES UNTIL DONE.

STUFFED EGGPLANT

2 OR 3 MED. EGGPLANTS	1 GREEN PEPPER	1 CUP WATER
1 LB. GROUND MEAT	1 CUP TOMATOES	½ TEAS. PEPPER
3 MED. ONIONS	1 STICK BUTTER	2 GARLIC CLOVES
2 TAB. CHOP PARSLEY	½ CAN TOMATO PASTE	2 TEAS. SALT
¼ TEAS. ACCENT	½ TEAS. PEPPER	

CUT IN HALF, REMOVE CENTER AND BRUSH INSIDES WITH BUTTER, SALT & PEPPER, BAKE IN 350 DEGREE OVEN FOR 20 MIN. MELT BUTTER IN SKILLET, ADD CHOP ONIONS, PEPPERS AND CHOP CENTER OF EGGPLANT, COOK FOR FIVE MIN. THEN ADD PASTE WITH WATER AND SALT, PEPPER. SEASON. SIMMER FOR 5 MIN. USE ANOTHER SKILLET, MELT BUTTER . ADD MEAT, SALT , PEPPER AND COOK FOR 5 MIN. THEN ADD SOME OF THE SAUTE TO MEAT, BLEND WELL, ADD PARSLEY, THEN FILL EACH HALF OF EGGPLANT WITH MEAT MIXTURE. SPREAD TOMATOES ON TOP, SEASON WITH SALT, PEPPER AND OIL; COVER DISH AND BAKE IN OVEN 350 DEGREES FOR 1 HOUR. SERVE 4 TO 6.

EGGPLANT NO. 4

1 LARGE EGGPLANT	3 MED ONIONS	½ STICK BUTTER
2 GARLIC CLOVES	¼ CUP TOASTED CRUMBS	½ GREEN PEPPER
1/8 TEAS. PAPRIKA	1/8 TEAS. CINNAMON	SALT & PEPPER

PEEL AND SLICE EGGPLANT. SPRINKLE ON SALT AND LET SET FOR 10 MIN. HEAT BUTTER IN SKILLET, ADD ONIONS, PEPPER AND GARLIC. COVER SKILLET AND COOK ON LOW FLAME UNTIL TENDER. DRAIN EGGPLANT, CUT IN PIECES, ADD

TWO ONIONS AND ALL SEASONINGS. COOK UNTIL DONE. ADD WATER IF NEEDED, THEN BLEND IN TOASTED CRUMBS, SIMMER FOR 5 MIN. SERVE 2 TO 4.

BAKED OKRA

1 LB. OKRA	½ STICK BUTTER
3 MED. ONIONS	SALT AND PEPPER
1 GARLIC CLOVE	4 TOMATOES (OR ½ C. TOMATO PASTE)
1 GREEN PEPPER	DASH OF CINNAMON

HEAT BUTTER IN SKILLET. ADD CHOPPED ONIONS, PEPPER AND GARLIC; BROWN SLIGHTLY. ADD TOMATOES OR MIX TOMATO PASTE WITH WATER HALF CUP, COOK ON LOW FLAME FOR 10 MINUTES. CLEAN OKRA, CUT OFF STEM-END, BUT NOT TOO CLOSE, PLACE IN ROASTER, SEASON, AND POUR THE SAUCE OVER IT. COVER AND COOK IN OVEN (350) UNTIL OKRA IS DONE.

BOILED CORN

6 EARS (OR MORE)	FEW DASHES OF BLACK PEPPER
SALT TO TASTE	½ STICK BUTTER (OR ½ C. MAZOLA)
FEW DASHES PAPRIKA	DASH OF TURMERIC

CLEAN CORN, PUT IN POT, ADD SEASONINGS AND ABOUT A C. OF WATER. COVER POT TIGHTLY AND STEAM OVER MED. FLAME UNTIL DONE.

CABBAGES

2-3 LB. CABBAGE HEAD	½ C. WATER	DASH OF PAPRIKA
1/3 C. OIL OR LESS	½ GREEN PEPPER	DASH OF TURMERIC
1 MED. ONION	SALT & PEPPER	

CLEAN, PUT IN POT, ADD SEASONINGS, NO WATER. COVER TIGHTLY AND STEAM OVER LOW FLAME UNTIL DONE, ADD SOME WATER IF NEEDED.

ACORN SQUASH PIE

2 C. COOKED SQUASH	1 STICK BUTTER
1½ C. SUGAR	1½ C. MILK

3 EGG YOLKS   DASH OF CINNAMON
2 TAB. FLOUR   NUTMEG AND FLAVOR

PEEL AND COOK SQUASH, MASH AND MEASURE. PUT IN BOWL, ADD ALL INGREDIENTS, AND MIX WELL. POUR IN <u>UNBAKED</u> PIE SHELL AND BAKE IN OVEN (375°) UNTIL NICELY BROWN.

APPLE PIE
(10-INCH PLATE)

2 LBS. APPLES	1½ OR 2 C. SUGAR	1/8 TEAS. NUTMEG
3 TAB. FLOUR	½ C. RAISINS	1/8 TEAS. CINNAMON
1 STICK BUTTER	½ C. WATER	PINCH OF SALT

PEEL AND SLICE APPLES, PUT IN POT, MIX SUGAR AND FLOUR, POUR OVER APPLES, AND MIX. ADD WATER AND COOK ON FLAME UNTIL TENDER. REMOVE FROM FLAME, ADD OTHER INGREDIENTS AND POUR INTO <u>UNBAKED</u> PIE CRUST. TOP WITH CROSS STRIPS OR WHOLE CRUST. PUT HOLES IN CRUST TO LET OUT STEAM. BAKE IN OVEN (350°) UNTIL BROWN.

APPLE COBBLER

USE SAME METHOD AS FOR PLATE PIE, RAISINS CAN BE OMITTED AND ADD MORE WATER AND USE THE BAKED STRIPS FOR COBBLER.

BUTTERMILK PIE

4 EGG YOLKS	1¼ C. SUGAR	1/8 TAES. NUTMEG
1 STICK BUTTER	1½ TEAS. VANILLA	1 TEAS. BAKING POWDER
2 TAB. FLOUR	½ C. CRUSH PINEAPPLE	PINCH OF SODA
2 C. MILK		

CREAM BUTTER AND SUGAR, ADD FLOUR AND EGG YOLK, MIX WELL. ADD OTHER INGREDIENTS AND MIX WELL. POUR IN <u>UNBAKED</u> PIE CRUST, BAKE IN OVEN (350°) ABOUT 1 HOUR OR UNTIL WELL SET. REMOVE FROM OVEN AND TOP WITH MERINGUE, RETURN TO OVER AND BROWN TO YOUR DESIRE.

CARROT PIE

1½ C. MASHED CARROTS	1 CAN EVAPORATED MILK
1 STICK BUTTER	3 EGGS
2 TAB. FLOUR	NUTMEG
1 C. SUGAR	VANILLA FLAVOR

PUT MASHED CARROTS IN BOWL, ADD BUTTER, FLOUR, SUGAR, EGGS, FLAVORS AND MILK, MIX WELL. POUR IN AN UNBAKED PIE CRUST, AND BAKE IN OVEN (400°) UNTIL NICELY BROWN. USE MERINGUE TOPPING, IF DESIRED.

CARROT CAKE

2 C. SUGAR	1½ C. VEG. OIL	3 C. FINELY GRATED CARROTS
4 EGGS	1½ TEAS. SODA	2 TEAS. CINNAMON
2 C. FLOUR	½ TEAS. SALT	

MIX OIL, SUGAR & EGGS. SIFT FLOUR, CINNAMON, SALT & SODA. ADD CARROTS & MIX WELL; POUR INTO LARGE PAN; BAKE AT 350° FOR 40 MINS. IF A GLASS PAN IS USED, BAKE AT 325°.

POUND CAKE

1 LB. BUTTER	6 EGGS	3 C. SIFTED CAKE FLOUR
1 LB. POWDER SUGAR	VANILLA AND LEMON EXTRACT	

CREAM BUTTER AND SUGAR. ADD EGGS ONE AT A TIME, BEATING ½ MIN. AFTER EACH EGG. ADD EXTRACT. ADD FLOUR 1 C. AT A TIME. BAKE AT 350° FOR ONE HOUR & 15 MINS.

WHITE POTATO PIE

1½ CUP MASHED POTATOES	2 TAB. FLOUR	3 EGGS
1 STICK BUTTER	1 CUP SUGAR	1 CAN PET OR CARNATION
PINCH SALT	NUTMEG	VANILLA

PUT POTATOES IN BOWL. ADD BUTTER, SUGAR, FLOUR, EGGS, MILK, SALT AND FLAVOR. MIX WELL AND POUR IN AN UNBAKED PIE CRUST AND BAKE IN OVEN

(400°) FOR 36 MIN. LOWER TEMPERATURE TO 350° AND CONTINUE TO COOK UNTIL NICELY BROWNED.

FISH CHILI

SAUTE: GARLIC, ONIONS, BELL PEPPERS, CELERY TO TASTE.
PRE-COOK: PINK OR NAVY BEANS (PINK BEST SUITED FOR THIS RECIPE.)
ADD: TOMATO JUICE, BLACK PEPPER, ACCENT, LAWRY'S SALT (SEASONED SALT), SALT, CHILI POWDER, CHILI-O-MIX.
ADD: SAUTEED VEGETABLES; LET SIMMER.
BROIL: IN OPEN PAN BROIL FISH IN SMALL AMOUNT OF OIL UNTIL FLAKY, NOT DRY. NEX FISH TO CHILI AND BEANS.

BROWNED CHICKEN

1 FRYER	1 STICK OF BUTTER	2 TAB. FLOUR
2 MED. ONIONS	OR OIL	2 STEMS CELERY
1 GARLIC CLOVE	½ GREEN PEPPER	1 TEAS. PAPRIKA
SALT AND PEPPER	¼ TEAS. LAWRY SALT	

CUT CHICKEN IN SERVINGS. SEASON WITH PAPRIKA, SALT, PEPPER AND TURMERIC AND SPRINKLE WITH WHITE FLOUR. MELT BUTTER IN ROASTER, BASTE CHICKEN AND LET IT BROWN IN OVEN (450 DEGREES). DRAIN OFF OIL AND ADD CHOPPED VEGETABLES AND ADD 1 OR 2 CUPS OF HOT WATER. COVER THE ROASTER, RETURN TO OVEN AND COOK AT 300 DEGREES UNTIL CHICKEN IS WELL DONE. ADD MORE WATER IF NEEDED. SERVE 4 TO 6.

CHICKEN WITH SAUCE

USE SAME INGREDIENTS AS FOR BROWNED CHICKEN, BUT USE ABOUT 2 TAB. TOMATO PASTE.
CLEAN CHICKEN AND CUT IN SERVINGS; SPRINKLE SALT, PEPPER AND FLOUR OVER CHICKEN. MELT BUTTER IN SKILLET, ADD CHICKEN AND BROWN IT SLIGHTLY. REMOVE FROM SKILLET, PLACE IN ROASTER, THEN ADD TO SKILLET CHOPPED ONIONS, GARLIC, PEPPER AND CELERY. COOK FOR ABOUT 10 MIN. THEN ADD

PASTE AND ABOUT 2 CUPS OF WATER, POUR IT OVER CHICKEN, COVER ROASTER AND COOK IN OVEN (350 DEGREES) UNTIL WELL DONE.

MEAT

MINUTE STEAK: MINUTE STEAK MAY BE BROILED, BUT IT IS GENERALLY PAN BROILED. HEAT A HEAVY FRYING PAN UNTIL SIZZLING HOT. SEAR THE STEAKS QUICKLY ON BOTH SIDES, LOWER THE HEAT AND COOK 2 MIN. ON EACH SIDE. REMOVE TO A HOT PLATTER, SPREAD WITH SOFTENED BUTTER, AND SPRINKLE WITH VEGETABLE SALT AND PAPRIKA. GARNISH WITH PARSLEY.

ELEGANT STEAK FOR PARTIES: GET A SIRLOIN OR PORTERHOUSE STEAK CUT 1½ TO 2 INCHES THICK. PUT A CUP OF FRENCH DRESSING IN A BOWL AND ADD A BAY LEAF AND A TBSP OF WORCESTERSHIRE SAUCE TO THE DRESSING. RUB THE STEAK ALL OVER WITH A GASHED CLOVE OF GARLIC, PUT IT IN A SHALLOW PAN OR A DEEP PLATTER. POUR THE DRESSING OVER IT AND LET IT MARINATE FOR AT LEAST AN HOUR, TURNING IT TWICE. PREHEAT THE BROILER FOR 10 MINUTES AND PUT THE STEAK UNDER THE HEAT WITH LOTS OF DRESSING CLINGING TO IT. SEAR QUICKLY ON BOTH SIDES, THEN REDUCE THE FLAME AND BROIL MORE SLOWLY. MEANWHILE SAUTE A POUND OF SLICED FRESH MUSHROOMS IN BUTTER AND TAKE THEM OUT OF THE SKILLET. PUT INTO THE SAME BUTTER SLICES OF GREEN PEPPER AND PIMENTO AND SAUTE THEM. PUT THE STEAK ON A PLATTER. SPRINKLE WITH VEGETABLE SALT, COVER WITH MUSHROOMS, AND GARNISH THE TOP WITH THE RED AND GREEN SLICES OF PIMENTO AND PEPPER. THIS IS A RECIPE WHERE YOU HAVE TO WORK FAST TO HAVE EVERYTHING PIPING HOT AT THE CRUCIAL MOMENT, BUT IT'S WELL WORTH IT FOR OCCASIONAL TIMES WHEN YOU FEEL AMBITIOUS.

BEEF STEW

2 LB. LEAN BEEF CUT IN 1-INCH CUBES	8 SMALL WHITE ONIONS
2 TBSP PURE VEGETABLE SHORTENING	8 UNPEELED CARROTS
1 LARGE ONION, CHOPPED	8 SMALL POTATOES

WATER	4 SMALL TURNIPS, CUT IN QUARTERS
3 STALKS CELERY, LEAVES AND ALL, CHOPPED	2 TBSP WHOLE WHEAT FLOUR

CUT THE MEAT INTO CUBES IF THE BUTCHER HASN'T ALREADY DONE IT. MELT THE SHORTENING IN A HEAVY IRON KETTLE--A DUTCH OVEN IF YOU HAVE ONE. SPRINKLE THE MEAT WITH VEGETABLE SALT AND BROWN IT IN THE FAT WITH THE CHOPPED ONION. (IF YOU PREFER NOT TO BROWN YOUR MEAT FIRST, ADD WATER IMMEDIATELY.) ADD ENOUGH HOT WATER SO IT ALMOST BUT NOT QUITE COVERS THE MEAT. COVER AND SIMMER SLOWLY OVER LOW HEAT FOR 2 HOURS, OR UNTIL THE MEAT IS ALMOST DONE. ADD THE WHOLE ONIONS, CARROTS, POTATOES, AND QUARTERED TURNIPS. CONTINUE SIMMERING ANOTHER HALF HOUR. REMOVE THE MEAT AND VEGETABLES TO A PLATTER. THICKEN THE LIQUID IN THE KETTLE WITH THE 2 TBSP. OF FLOUR MIXED TO A SMOOTH PASTE WITH A LITTLE COLD WATER. SERVE THE GRAVY EITHER OVER THE STEW OR IN A SEPARATE DISH.

BARBECUE SAUCE

1 CAN TOMATO PASTE	2 TBSP NATURAL BROWN SUGAR
1½ C. WARM WATER	¼ C. FINELY CHOPPED ONION
½ C. LEMON JUICE	½ CLOVE GARLIC, FINELY CHOPPED
4 TSP WORCESTERSHIRE SAUCE	½ TSP SALT
½ TSP VEGETABLE SALT	½ TSP CHILI POWDER

MIX ALL THE INGREDIENTS IN A SAUCEPAN. BRING TO A BOIL, REDUCE THE HEAT, THEN SIMMER 20 MINUTES, STIRRING FREQUENTLY. 2 CUPS, ENOUGH FOR A 5 POUND ROAST.

OUTDOOR BARBECUING IS SUGGESTED FOR THE FOLLOWING RECIPES; HOWEVER, AN INDOOR BROILER-ROTISSERIE CAN BE SUBSTITUTED. YOU CAN ALSO BAKE THE FOLLOWING SLOWLY IN A MODERATE OVEN. THE TASTE WILL BE SOMEWHAT DIFFERENT THAN THAT PRODUCED BY COALS, BUT WILL BE EQUALLY AS TASTY.

BARBECUED CHICKEN OR TURKEY: CUT YOUNG FRYERS ABOUT 1½ TO 2½ POUNDS IN HALVES OR QUARTERS. LET STAND IN ANY BARBECUE SAUCE SEVERAL HOURS. GRILL OVER HOT COALS SLOWLY ABOUT 50 TO 60 MINUTES. BASTE OFTEN. YOUNG 3 TO 6 POUND TURKEY BROILERS ARE COOKED THE SAME AS CHICKEN, BROIL 1½ TO 2 HOURS. CHICKEN OR TURKEY MAY BE BROILED WITHOUT FIRST PLACING IN MARINADE. FOWL IS BRUSHED WITH MELTED BUTTER OR OIL; SEASON WITH SALT AND PEPPER; BROWN ON ALL SIDES. BRUSH WITH BARBECUE SAUCE OR MELTED BUTTER AND LEMON JUICE OR GARLIC.

GRILLED LAMB CHOPS: SELECT CHOPS OR LAMB STEAKS 1 TO 2 INCHES THICK. MARINATE IN ANY BARBECUE SAUCE 30 TO 40 MINUTES. COOK THE SAME AS STEAK, BRUSHING WITH SAUCE AS THEY COOK. 1 INCH CHOPS, MEDIUM-WELL DONE WILL TAKE ABOUT 10 TO 15 MINUTES ON EACH SIDE.

BARBECUED HOT DOGS (ALL BEEF): CUT HOT DOGS LENGTHWISE, ALMOST THROUGH BUT NOT QUITE, AND SPREAD CUT SIDES WITH MUSTARD OR THICK BARBECUE SAUCE. ARRANGE ON GRILLED SIDE DOWN, TURN TO BROWN EVENLY. COOK 5 TO 10 MINUTES.

BARBECUED FLANK STEAK: FOR 6 PERSONS BUY 2 FLANK STEAKS. LAY FLAT AND SCORE 1 SIDE OR ASK THE BUTCHER TO DO IT. DICE 1 C. ONIONS AND MIX WITH ½ C. MINCED PARSLEY. SPRINKLE LIBERALLY OVER STEAKS. ROLL EACH PIECE TIGHTLY; TIE ROLLS WITH TWINE AND SLIP ON SPIT. COOK 1½ HOURS OVER MEDIUM FIRE. SERVE BY CUTTING AS FOR JELLY ROLL.

BARBECUED BEEF HEART: ASK BUTCHER TO CUT A BEEF HEART SO IT LIES FLAT. REMOVE FAT AND HARD TISSUE. INTERLACE ON SPIT AS YOU WOULD FOR SPARE RIBS. BRUSH LIGHTLY WITH OIL. COOK 1¼ HOURS OVER MEDIUM HEAT AND HEART WILL BE TENDER AND JUICY.

CHICKEN GRILLED WITH SOY SAUCE: HAVE 2 FRYING CHICKENS SPLIT IN HALF; SPRINKLE EACH HALF WITH LIBERALLY WITH SOY SAUCE AND MARINATE IN THE SOY SAUCE 1 HOUR. WORK EXCESS SAUCE INTO CHICKEN BY RUBBING. PLACE ON GRILL, SKIN SIDE DOWN, OVER MEDIUM HEAT FOR 20 MINUTES. TURN, AND IF POSSIBLE, COVER WITH LARGE PAN. COOK 20 MINUTES; REMOVE PAN, TURN THE

CHICKEN AGAIN AND COOK 15 MORE MINUTES. IF USING WHOLE CHICKENS ON SPIT, RUB SOY SAUCE INTO BIRD. SPRINKLE CAVITY AND COOK AS USUAL. DO NOT USE SALT OR PEPPER IN EITHER METHOD.

BEEF KABOBS

1½ LBS. BEEF, CUT 1½ IN. THICK (CHUCK, SIRLOIN OR ROUND)

1 CLOVE GARLIC, MINCED

3 TBSP SALAD OIL

¼ TSP DRY MUSTARD

1½ TBSP SOY SAUCE

½ TSP ROSEMARY, CRUSHED

½ C. VINEGAR

1 TBSP WORCESTERSHIRE SAUCE

1 TBSP MEAT SAUCE

½ C. CATSUP

ONIONS, GREEN PEPPERS, TOMATOES OR MUSHROOMS

CUT MEAT INTO 1 INCH SQUARES AND PLACE IN SHALLOW DISH. SPRINKLE MEAT WITH MONOSODIUM GLUTAMATE IF DESIRED. SAUTE GARLIC IN OIL. BLEND IN MUSTARD, SOY SAUCE, ROSEMARY AND VINEGAR. POUR MIXTURE OVER CUT MEAT. PLACE IN REFRIGERATOR TO MARINATE AND CHILL FOR 24 HOURS. TURN MEAT OCCASIONALLY. ARRANGE CHUNKS OF MEAT ON SKEWERS ALTERNATELY WITH PIECES OF ONION, GREEN PEPPER AND TOMATO. PLACE FILLED SKEWERS ON COLD BROILER GRID. TO REMAINING MARINADE, ADD CATSUP AND WORCESTERSHIRE SAUCE AND BRUSH MEAT AND VEGETABLES ON SKEWERS GENEROUSLY WITH THIS SAUCE. PLACE BROILER PAN WITH KABOBS IN BROILER COMPARTMENT, WITH TOP OF MEAT AND VEGETABLES 3 INCHES FROM TIP OF BROILER FLAME. BROIL FOR 5 TO 8 MINUTES. TURN. BRUSH WITH SAUCE AGAIN. BROIL FOR 5 TO 8 MINUTES ON SECOND SIDE. BROILING TIME DEPENDS ON THICKNESS OF MEAT, AMOUNT OF BROWNING DESIRED AND DEGREE OF DONENESS PREFERRED.

LEMON CHUCK STEAK

1 CHUCK STEAK, CUT 1½ INCHES THICK (ABOUT 5 LBS)	1½ TSP SALT
1 TSP GRATED LEMON PEEL	1/8 TSP PEPPER
2/3 C. LEMON JUICE	1 TSP WORCESTERSHIRE SAUCE
1/3 C. SALAD OIL	1 TSP PREPARED MUSTARD
2 TSP MONOSODIUM GLUTAMATE	2 GREEN ONION TOPS, SLICED

SCORE FAT EDGES OF MEAT. PLACE IN SHALLOW DISH. COMBINE REMAINING INGREDIENTS; POUR OVER STEAK. LET STAND 3 HOURS AT ROOM TEMPERATURE OR 6 HOURS IN REFRIGERATOR, TURNING STEAK SEVERAL TIMES. REMOVE STEAK FROM MARINADE; WITH PAPER TOWELING, REMOVE EXCESS MOISTURE. COOK OVER HOT COALS ABOUT 12 MINUTES ON EACH SIDE FOR MEDIUM FOR RARE OR 15 MINUTES ON EACH SIDE FOR MEDIUM OR ABOUT 20 MINUTES ON EACH SIDE FOR WELL DONE. BRUSH OCCASIONALLY WITH THE MARINADE. CARVE MEAT ACROSS GRAIN IN THIN SLICES.

SWANK PORTERHOUSE: SLASH FAT EDGE ON ONE 2½ TO 3 POUND PORTERHOUSE OR SIRLOIN STEAK (ABOUT 2 INCHES THICK). SLITTING FROM FAT SIDE, CUT POCKET IN EACH SIDE OF LEAN, CUTTING ALMOST TO THE BONE. COMBINE ¾ C. FINELY CHOPPED BERMUDA ONION, 2 CLOVES GARLIC, MINCED; DASH SALT, DASH PEPPER AND DASH CELERY SALT. STUFF INTO STEAK POCKETS. MIX 3 TBSP CLARET AND 2 TBSP SOY SAUCE; BRUSH ON STEAK. BROIL OVER HOT COALS A TOTAL OF 35 MINUTES OR TILL DONE TO YOUR LIKING, TURNING ONCE. BRUSH OCCASIONALLY WITH SOY MIXTURE. HEAT ¼ C. BUTTER AND ONE 3-OUNCE CAN SLICED MUSHROOMS, DRAINED; POUR OVER STEAK. SLICE ACROSS GRAIN.

GRILLED RIB EYE ROAST: HAVE A 5 TO 6 POUND BEEF RIB EYE ROAST TIED WITH STRING AT 1½ INCH INTERVALS. CENTER MEAT ON SPIT; FASTEN WITH HOLDING FORKS. ATTACH SPIT: TURN ON MOTOR. HAVE HOT COALS AT BACK OF FIREBOX AND DRIP PAN UNDER ROAST. ROAST 3 TO 3½ HOURS FOR MEDIUM-WELL OR TO YOUR LIKING. MEAT THERMOMETER WILL REGISTER 140 DEG. FOR RARE, 160 DEG.

FOR MEDIUM AND 170 DEG. FOR WELL DONE. LET STAND 15 MINUTES BEFORE CARVING. SERVE WITH HERB BUTTER; BLEND ½ C. SOFTENED BUTTER WITH 2 TSP. SEASONED SALT, 1 TSP FINE HERBS, ½ TSP FRESHLY GROUND PEPPER AND FEW DROPS BOTTLED HOT PEPPER SAUCE. DAB A LITTLE ON EACH SERVING OF MEAT.

BUTTERFLY LEG OF LAMB

1 5-TO-6 POUND LEG OF LAMB

½ TSP DRIED THYME, CRUSHED

1 OR 2 CLOVES GARLIC, MINCED

½ C. GRATED ONION

1 TSP SALT

½ C. SALAD OIL

1 TSP FINE HERBS

½ C. LEMON JUICE

½ TSP PEPPER

HAVE BUTCHER BONE LEG OF LAMB AND SLIT LENGTHWISE TO SPREAD FLAT LIKE A THICK STEAK. IN LARGE GLASS DISH OR BAKING PAN, THOROUGHLY BLEND REMAINING INGREDIENTS. PLACE MEAT IN MARINADE. LEAVE AT LEAST ONE HOUR AT ROOM TEMPERATURE, OR OVERNIGHT IN THE REFRIGERATOR, TURNING OCCASIONALLY. REMOVE MEAT AND RESERVE MARINADE. INSERT 2 LONG SKEWERS THROUGH MEAT AT RIGHT ANGLES MAKING AN X OR PLACE MEAT IN A WIRE BASKET. THIS WILL MAKE FOR EASY TURNING OF THE MEAT AND KEEP MEAT FROM CURLING DURING COOKING. ROAST OVER MEDIUM COALS 1½ TO 2 HOURS TURNING EVERY 15 MINUTES TILL MEDIUM OR WELL DONE. BASTE FREQUENTLY WITH RESERVED MARINADE. REMOVE SKEWERS AND CUT ACROSS GRAIN INTO THIN SLICES.

BARBECUE MEAT LOAVES

2 LBS. GROUND BEEF

½ TSP DRY MUSTARD

2 SLIGHTLY BEATEN EGGS

¼ C. MILK

2 C. SOFT WHOLE WHEAT BREAD CRUMBS

½ C. BUTTER OR MARGARINE

¼ C. FINELY CHOPPED ONION

½ C. CATSUP

1 TBSP PREPARED HORSERADISH	1½ TSP SALT

COMBINE FIRST 8 INGREDIENTS AND MIX WELL. SHAPE IN MINIATURE MEAT LOAVES ABOUT 4½ X 2½ INCHES. HEAT BUTTER WITH CATSUP JUST UNTIL BUTTER MELTS. BRUSH OVER ALL SIDES OF LOAVES. COOK MEAT LOAVES OVER MEDIUM COALS; TURN AND BRUSH ALL SIDES FREQUENTLY WITH SAUCE. COOK 40 MINUTES OR TILL DONE. PASS REMAINING SAUCE.

MARINATED DRUMSTICKS

½ C. CATSUP	¼ C. SALAD OIL
2 TO 3 TSP LEMON JUICE	½ TSP MONOSODIUM GLUTAMATE
2 TBSP SOY SAUCE	12 CHICKEN DRUMSTICKS

COMBINE FIRST 5 INGREDIENTS, MIXING WELL. ADD CHICKEN LEGS AND TURN TO COAT. REFRIGERATE OVERNIGHT, SPOONING MARINADE OVER OCCASIONALLY. PLACE DRUMSTICKS IN WIRE BROILER BASKET. BROIL OVER MEDIUM COALS FOR ABOUT 1 HOUR OR TILL TENDER, TURNING OCCASIONALLY. BASTE WITH MARINADE NOW AND THEN.

GRILLED TURKEY PIECES

1 6-TO-7 POUND READY-TO-COOK TURKEY	1 TSP GROUND GINGER
¼ C. SALAD OIL	1 TSP DRY MUSTARD
¼ C. SOY SAUCE	1 TSP MONOSODIUM GLUTAMATE
1 TBSP HONEY	1 CLOVE GARLIC, MINCED

CUT TURKEY IN PIECES AS FOLLOWS: 2 WINGS, 2 DRUMSTICKS, 2 THIGHS, 4 BREAST PIECES AND 2 BACK PIECES. COMBINE REMAINING INGREDIENTS FOR MARINADE. PLACE TURKEY PIECES IN MARINADE ABOUT 2 HOURS AT ROOM TEMPERATURE OR OVERNIGHT IN THE REFRIGERATOR. PLACE PIECES ON GRILL 6 TO 8 INCHES ABOVE MEDIUM HOT COALS. (ADD WINGS AND BACK ½ HOUR

LATER). BROIL, TURNING OCCASIONALLY, 1 HOUR. BASTE WITH MARINADE; BROIL 30 MINUTES. TEST FOR DONENESS, CUT INTO DRUMSTICK--NO PINK NEAR BONE.

HICKORY FISH

2 POUNDS FISH FILLETS	¼ C. BUTTER, MELTED
1 LEMON, THINLY SLICED	1 CLOVE GARLIC, MINCED

SPRINKLE FISH GENEROUSLY WITH SALT AND PEPPER. ARRANGE HALF THE LEMON SLICES IN BOTTOM OF A SHALLOW BAKING PAN; ADD FISH IN SINGLE LAYER. PLACE REMAINING LEMON ATOP. COMBINE BUTTER AND GARLIC; POUR OVER FISH. ADD HICKORY TO SLOW COALS. PLACE BAKING PAN ATOP GRILL. CLOSE HOOD AND COOK 25 TO 30 MINUTES, BASTING FREQUENTLY. SERVE WITH THE LEMON SLICES AND BUTTER MIXTURE.

HUNGARIAN GOULASH

2 LB LEAN BEEF CUT IN 1-INCH CUBES	2 CLOVES GARLIC, MINCED
2 TBSP PURE VEGETABLE SHORTENING	1 TSP SALT
4 ONIONS, CHOPPED	1 TSP PAPRIKA
½ TSP CARAWAY SEEDS	2 C. CUBED POTATOES
1 BAY LEAF	2 C. STRAINED TOMATOES

CUT THE MEAT IN CUBES IF THE BUTCHER HASN'T DONE IT ALREADY--AND BY THE WAY, YOU MAY USE HALF VEAL AND HALF BEEF IN THIS RECIPE IF YOU PREFER. MELT THE SHORTENING IN A HEAVY IRON KETTLE OR DUTCH OVEN AND BROWN THE MEAT WITH THE CHOPPED ONION AND GARLIC. ADD THE SALT, PAPRIKA, BAY LEAF AND CARAWAY SEEDS. HEAT THE TOMATOES AND POUR THEM OVER THE MEAT. COVER TIGHTLY AND SIMMER OVER A LOW HEAT ABOUT 2 HOURS, UNTIL THE MEAT IS TENDER. ADD MORE TOMATOES AS NEEDED. ADD THE POTATOES A HALF HOUR BEFORE THE MEAT IS DONE. IF DESIRED, THICKEN THE GRAVY WITH 2 TBSP WHOLE WHEAT FLOUR MIXED WITH A LITTLE COLD WATER.

BEEF STROGANOFF

2 LB LEAN BEEF CUT IN 1-INCH CUBES	1 TBSP CHOPPED PARSLEY
2/3 C. SEASONED WHOLE WHEAT FLOUR	½ PT. SOUR CREAM OR YOGURT
2 TBSP VEGETABLE SHORTENING	1 TBSP SOY SAUCE
1 LARGE ONION, SLICED	½ TSP SALT
½ LB MUSHROOMS, SLICED	PAPRIKA TO TASTE
2 C. HOT WATER	

CUT THE MEAT INTO CUBES IF THE BUTCHER HASN'T ALREADY DONE IT. DREDGE IT IN SEASONED WHOLE WHEAT FLOUR. MELT THE SHORTENING IN A HEAVY SKILLET OR DUTCH OVEN. BROWN THE MEAT WITH THE ONIONS AND MUSHROOMS. ADD THE HOT WATER, COVER TIGHTLY, AND SIMMER SLOWLY OVER LOW HEAT UNTIL TENDER--ABOUT 2 HOURS. REMOVE THE COVER DURING THE LAST PART OF THE COOKING AND LET THE LIQUID COOK DOWN TO ABOUT HALF THE QUANTITY. FIVE MINUTES BEFORE SERVING, ADD PARSLEY, POUR SOUR CREAM OR YOGURT AND SOY SAUCE. TASTE AND SEASON TO SUIT WITH SALT AND PAPRIKA.

SWISS STEAK

PURCHASE 2 LBS. ROUND STEAK, 1 INCH THICK. PLACE ON BOARD AND SEASON WITH SALT, PEPPER AND OREGANO. SPRINKLE 2 TBSP FLOUR OVER STEAK AND POUND IN WITH SIDE OF SMALL PIE PAN. TURN ON OTHER SIDE AND REPEAT. PLACE 2 TBSP OIL IN SKILLET AND BROWN STEAK ON BOTH SIDES. HALF COVER STEAK WITH HOT WATER AND SIMMER 1½ HOURS. REMOVE STEAK TO HOT PLATTER, THICKEN LIQUID WITH A LITTLE FLOUR AND POUR OVER STEAK. SPRINKLE CHOPPED PARSLEY ALL OVER.

INDEX

WHOLE WHEAT BREAD	5
WHOLE WHEAT BREAD NO.2	6
WHOLE WHEAT BREAD NO.3	6
WHOLE WHEAT BREAD NO.4	7
WHOLE WHEAT PARKER ROLLS	8
PUMPERNICKEL, MOLASSES RYE BREAD	9
SOURDOUGH, WHOLE WHEAT EGG ROLLS	10
QUICK HOT ROLLS	11
HOT CROSS BUNS	12
WHOLE WHEAT BREAD NO.5, MUFFIN ROLLS	13
CLOVER LEAF ROLLS, BEAN SOUP, VEGETABLE SOUP	14
BARBECUED MEATS, BROWN RICE	15
BROWN RICE WITH VEGETABLES	16
SALADS	17
FACTS ABOUT SALADS	21
SALAD GREENS	23
TOSSED SALAD GREENS	24
MAYONNAISE	26
CHEESE, CHEESE SOUFFLE	28
CORN AND CHEESE SOUFFLE, CREOLE TOAST, CREAM CHEESE ICING	29
LOW-CALORIE STUFFED CELERY	30
LOW-CALORIE CHEESE-RICE CASSEROLE	30
CHEESE STUFFED APPLES	30
SQUASH CHEESE CASSEROLE, MEATLESS CHILI WITH CHEESE	31
CHEESE CROQUETTES	31
CHEESE SAUCE, CHEESE THINS	32
MEATLESS CHEESEBURGERS, OLIVE CHEESE TURNOVERS	33
CREAM CHEESE SAVOURIES	33
CHEESE AND OLIVES ON TOAST, PEPPERS WITH CHEESE	34
SOBER WELSH RAREBIT	34
EGGS	36

APPLE OMELET, EGG OMELET WITH SQUASH	38
RAGOUT OF EGGS	38
EGG CHOP SUEY, CHINESE EGGS	39
EGGS ON VEGGIE TOAST, POACHED EGGS DE LUXE	40
OMELET SOUFFLE	40
EGGS FLORENTINE, EGGS AND RICE CASSEROLE	41
CHOPPED OKRA, CAULIFLOWER, CAULIFLOWER NO.1	42
CAULIFLOWER NO.2, BAKED SUMMER SQUASH	43
STUFFED ZUCCHINI SQUASH	43
STUFFED CUCUMBERS, NO.1 ASPARAGUS CASSEROLE	44
NO.2 ASPARAGUS CASSEROLE, NO.3 PLAIN ASPARAGUS	45
EGGPLANT AND RICE CASSEROLE	45
BATTERED EGGPLANT, ROASTED EGGPLANT	46
STRING BEANS, STRING BEANS (EGYPTIAN STYLE)	47
GREEN PEAS WITH SAUCE	47
GREEN PEAS WITH POTATOES, BAKED ZUCCHINI WITH CHEESE	48
SUMMER SQUASH (WHITE, YELLOW OR GREEN)	48
ZUCCHINI STUFFED SQUASH, ARABIC STYLE	49
STUFFED CABBAGE	49
STUFFED PEPPERS, STUFFED EGGPLANT, EGGPLANT NO.4	50
BAKED OKRA, BOILED CORN, CABBAGES	51
ACORN SQUASH PIE, APPLE PIE, APPLE COBBLER, BUTTERMILK PIE	52
CARROT PIE, CARROT CAKE, POUND CAKE, WHITE POTATO PIE	53
FISH CHILI, BROWNED CHICKEN, CHICKEN WITH SAUCE	54
MEAT, BEEF STEW	55
BARBECUE SAUCE, BARBECUE MEATS	56
BEEF SHISH KABOBS, LEMON CHUCK STEAK, SWANK PORTERHOUSE	58
GRILLED RIBEYE STEAK	58
BUTTERFLY LEG OF LAMB, BARBECUE MEAT LOAVES	60
MARINATED DRUMSTICKS, GRILLED TURKEY PIECES	61
HICKORY FISH, HUNGARIAN GOULASH, BEEF STROGANOFF	62
SWISS STEAK	63